TOWARD MORNING

By Alta Halverson Seymour

Cover design by Tina DeKam
Cover illustration by Larissa Sharina
First published in 1961
© 2021 Jenny Phillips
goodandbeautiful.com

Chapters

Chapter One 1
Chapter Two 10
Chapter Three 20
Chapter Four 28
Chapter Five 37
Chapter Six 45
Chapter Seven 54
Chapter Eight 63
Chapter Nine 72
Chapter Ten 81
Chapter Eleven 89

Chapters

*To Anyuka, Sara, and Frank
with thanks for factual
help and friendship*

Chapter One

"WHAT ARE YOU going to do, Janos?" Teresa Nagy's eyes were anxious as she watched her tall brother pull on his coat and stand waiting at the sitting room window of their little apartment that October day in Budapest.

Janos had a tense, determined look that made Teresa sure something definite and probably dangerous was in the making. She had suspected it for several days—days when he had stayed longer than usual at the college, had brought home a group of young students to spend hours in his small room, talking, talking, talking in earnest voices.

"Hungary has got to strike for freedom, and there's no use waiting!" she had heard them say. "Eleven years they've bled Hungary, and that's enough! We can't stand this kind of tyranny any longer, and we're not going to!" Dangerous words, she knew that well enough. Janos and the boys were brave, but Teresa was very much afraid.

"The Poles have broken with Russia," Janos said to Teresa.

"We students have permission to show our sympathy by standing in front of the Polish embassy, if we don't make any noise! A wonderful permission, and more than likely they'll yank that away before we've stood there five minutes!"

Janos looked at his sister, his dark eyes full of fire, and she thought he was going to say something more. Then a hail from the street made him turn and give a wave in answer. "Here they are!" he said. With a quick farewell, he hurried down the stairs and out into the street.

Teresa stood for a moment watching. There were Artur Zelk, the brother of her best friend, Piroska; her cousin Stephan; and several other college students. Ferenc Zelk was there too, she noted with special interest. She had a great admiration for Ferenc, barely sixteen but so full of zeal and fire and ideas that the older boys often allowed him in their meetings.

They swung down the streets. Teresa shivered a little as she watched them. That permission—she didn't trust it, and it was plain Janos didn't either. She had the uneasy feeling that this whole affair was going to lead to trouble.

It was Teresa's job to keep the small apartment in order and prepare the meals, but today it seemed almost impossible for her to settle to any work. She felt restless and anxious and wished that her mother were at home.

"Anyuka" was what they called her—Little Mother. Janos had started it when he outstripped his mother in height, and the others had taken up the pet name. It fitted her well in some ways, but small and slender though she was, Anyuka had a quality of wiry strength and determination that had carried them all through more than one difficult time. Since their father's death, and until Janos was old enough to be of some assistance, she had supported the family with her dressmaking shop in Budapest. Now that Teresa was fourteen, she was learning to help there. As soon as her work in the apartment was finished, she would hurry down to the shop.

But Teresa didn't get to the shop that day. She was in the midst of the dishwashing when the door flew open and her twelve-year-old brother, Belo, burst in.

"Teresa, they took away permission—the Central Committee of the Communists—and the students are gathering in the colleges! I saw Janos—he was furious, and so were the others! He said the Committee didn't want any political demonstrations, but they're going to get one that will surprise them."

"What are they going to do?"

"I don't know for sure—but they're going to do something. I think they're going to march to Petofi Square. I'm going over to see. You'd better come too."

"The dishes—" murmured Teresa mechanically.

"Phooey! Who cares about dishes today? Come on!"

Belo dashed down the stairs. Teresa jerked on a coat and ran after him to the square named for Hungary's beloved patriot poet, Petofi, who had written stirring poems of liberation during the revolution of 1848.

People were coming from all directions, and as Teresa and Belo stood in the square waiting, they heard the sound of marching feet. Then down the street came columns of students, ten abreast, Janos in the first row.

A crowd had gathered now. Eyes were alert and watchful, but there was little noise as the columns of solemn-faced students came marching on. Suddenly from somewhere in the crowd came the shout, "We vow we can never be slaves!" That was a line everyone knew—a line from a Petofi poem. Someone began to sing the stirring "Kossuth Anthem," written by another hero of 1848. Others took it up till everyone was singing. Then came the "Marseillaise," and from the way the people sang, it was plain they meant every word. Song followed song; Teresa and Belo joined fervently in the singing. The urge for freedom spread like wildfire.

At first Teresa and Belo managed to stay together and even to keep Janos in sight. But as the crowd surged and pushed, they could no longer see Janos, and soon Teresa realized that she had lost Belo.

It was impossible to look for anyone, but as Teresa struggled to work her way to where she could again at least see Janos, a voice she knew spoke in her ear. "Come on, Teresa. Janos has work for us to do."

How Ferenc had reached her in that tightly packed, excited crowd, Teresa couldn't imagine, but somehow he had done it. That was Ferenc for you! "Zita'll meet us at your apartment," he said. "Come on. She's got a few hours' leave from the hospital. She knows what to do. So do I."

Zita, Janos' fiancée, was even now almost like one of the family. Teresa knew Janos placed great confidence in her.

Teresa's heart beat faster than ever at the thought that now she too was to have a real part in helping with whatever was afoot. She kept close to Ferenc as he worked his way to the edge of the crowd, and together they hurried homeward.

Zita was hard at work in the little sitting room, and Anyuka was there too, her thin intent face bent over a pile of narrow red, green, and white ribbons, while Zita glued placards to sticks.

"Hungary Wants Freedom!" "Give Us Back Our Church!" "Russians, Go Home!" were some of the slogans Teresa read.

"You can help me with these, Ferenc. They're doing a lot more over at your house, but your uncle and father and mother and Piroska are there to help," said Zita.

"They're doing them all over Budapest. Somehow the students got hold of a printing press and turned a lot out," answered Ferenc, setting at once to work.

Anyuka looked up, such hope and determination in her dark eyes that Teresa felt confidence and some of that same determination replacing the wild excitement and restlessness that had swept over her in the crowd.

"Come, Teresa, your fingers are quick. We are making armbands for all the patriots. Who knows what these red and white and green emblems will see in the next few days? We expect it to be Hungary's freedom."

"Listen! You can hear them singing and shouting!" cried Zita. "Oh, how I'd like to be with them!"

"You can be of more use right here at this minute," Anyuka said. "They want these placards and emblems just as soon as they can get them."

"I'll be carrying one!" Zita's voice was triumphant.

"Believe me, I will too," said Ferenc. "I wouldn't be here now, I can tell you, if they didn't want these in a hurry."

"I wish I knew where Belo was," said Anyuka. "He's so daring."

Everyone was relieved when Belo rushed in not long afterward shouting, "I'm to help! Janos and Artur are going to try to get back in an hour or so for the stuff. Janos sent me to tell you. Here, I can help glue!"

Everyone worked with feverish haste, and when Janos and Artur burst in, they found a pile of slogans and another of emblems ready.

"Come on, Ferenc. You too, Zita. We're going to pull down old Stalin's statue. The cadets and army officers have been coming out of the military academy to join us. We're sure some of the army is going to be with us. Come! You coming, Belo? You too, Teresa, Anyuka!"

"We have more emblems to make—" Anyuka began. Then she stood up. "But we can keep on with these all night if necessary. This is a sight we must see."

Janos and Zita, Ferenc and Belo, were flying on ahead of them, but Teresa and Anyuka were soon on the edge of the hurrying crowd.

Others too must have been working to good purpose, for placards were lifted high everywhere in the crowd, and the red, white, and green armbands appeared and were speedily fastened on sleeves.

The crowd, still singing, surged on. From somewhere came ropes, but the twenty-five-foot bronze statue of Stalin refused to budge. Then acetylene torches appeared, and cables and ladders. The statue gave at the knees, crashed, and people rushed to grab small pieces.

"There's Belo—you might know!" cried Teresa. "He's getting a piece for a souvenir."

"Good for him!" said a man near her. "That statue stood for slavery. This is only a beginning!"

Students and workers were tearing the Soviet hammer and sickle from Hungarian flags, pulling down Red stars from buildings—working with almost hysterical speed.

After that, things happened so fast, Teresa didn't know what would come next. News flew through the crowd that Party Leader Gero had spoken over Radio Budapest, condemning the demonstrations and the demands for freedom.

Someone up in front was speaking rapidly and distinctly and loud enough for all those around to hear. "We're going to the radio station!" he called out. "We're going to have our demands made public! We're going to tell the world the truth!"

On rushed the people, Teresa and Anyuka being swept along with the crowd. As they came to a halt in front of the radio station, there were angry murmurs, excited protests: "There are the Security Police!" "They're arresting the delegation!"

"Anyuka, do you think Janos was in that delegation?" Teresa

asked, her face very white. All Hungary knew what to expect from the dreaded Security Police.

Anyuka's face was white too; Teresa couldn't hear her answer. The crowd was rushing onward now, storming the building, and the police opened fire on them. A group of students were climbing up to the balcony in front of the building. Fighting had begun.

Suddenly Teresa heard the sharp zing of a bullet and felt a swift, stinging pain. Blood was running down her arm. For a moment she felt faint. Then a man nearby steadied her, and Anyuka's voice, sounding far away, said, "I must get her home."

"I don't want to go home! Not now!" Teresa tried to say. "We don't know about Janos."

But no one listened. The crowd made way for her, as they had made way for others wounded by those shots of the police. "Shooting children!" cried one. "Firing on an unarmed crowd!" exclaimed another.

Tearing her kerchief into strips, Anyuka bound up the arm as well as she could. One or two in the crowd, indignant and concerned, insisted on helping the two home.

"I wanted to stay," said Teresa, as Anyuka washed and bound the wound properly. "I wanted to see what happened to Janos."

"They'll let us know," Anyuka answered, though her face was tense. "Thank the Lord this is a flesh wound and will soon heal. You sleep now, Teresa."

"I don't want to sleep. I want to stay awake and know what's going on," objected Teresa. "I want to wait and watch with you."

But the excitement and pain and loss of blood had wearied her more than she knew, and in spite of herself, she fell asleep.

Suddenly she was wide awake. The apartment door had opened, and she heard her mother cry, "Oh, Janos! It's toward morning! I'd almost given up. You weren't arrested, then!"

"Not yet anyway. But oh, Mother, what a night! Trucks full of Hungarian soldiers came in and tanks manned by Hungarians. But the soldiers and students and workers are all together. When a tank came rumbling in, we didn't know what to expect, but then a wonderful thing happened. A Hungarian colonel stood up in the hatch and called out, 'We came to join you, not to oppose you.' At least part of the army is with us. We've got Tommy guns. We're building barricades in the street. This is revolution!"

Revolution it was. In those feverish days and nights that followed so swiftly, Teresa's job was to help Anyuka somehow keep food ready for the boys who used their house as headquarters. Often it was difficult to find even the makings of soup. Teresa was impatient many times with her arm, which kept her from working as fast as she wanted to; but she managed as well as she could in spite of it. Others, she knew, had fared far worse. The boys coming in for food or snatches of sleep told of many killed or wounded. Russian tanks rumbled into the city; machine guns were busy night and day.

But wary and tense as the boys were, and sad to report wounded and dead, they were hopeful and even confident of the outcome.

After days and nights of fighting, Artur and Janos and Ferenc burst in, faces grimy from the fighting, but eyes fairly blazing with triumph. "The Soviet tanks are pulling out!" they shouted. "They've promised to negotiate with us. They've promised us freedom!"

For five jubilant days, Hungary was free. Students and workers toiled side by side trying to get the ravaged city into some kind of order. Streets were clogged with rubble and glass, uprooted cobblestones, wrecked tanks. "There's a lot for us to do," said Janos, but his eyes shone. "And we're the ones who can do it."

On All Saints' Day, for the first time in many years, there was a spirit of joy in the city. Country folk came to town with gifts of geese and ducks, vegetables and fruit. Teresa helped her mother prepare such a feast as they had not seen for many a long day. Candles burned all over the city. In the square where the soldiers had fired into the crowd, a thousand candles made a circle.

"What a Sunday it will be!" exulted Teresa. "Let's have a lot of folks in!"

"We've been having a lot of folks right along," said Anyuka, smiling, "but this could be a real party, Teresa. That's what you want, isn't it?"

But Saturday night Janos came in, looking very sober. "I don't like what I hear," he said. "They say they're negotiating, but I'm not so sure. Soviet troops are pouring into Hungary. They say it's just to keep the peace, but we don't need them. We can have peace better without them."

Early Sunday morning, he awakened the family. "It's happened," he said, his face grim. "They've tricked us. They've opened fire on Budapest. Tanks are pouring into the city. I'm going."

Anyuka's face was as stern as his. "I'm going too. I'd better get right to the hospital where Zita is," she said. "I'll be needed there."

"Janos," whispered Teresa, as he bent to kiss her goodbye, "come back as soon as you can."

"I'll come back if I can, Tessa," said Janos. "If I don't, you'd better get to the shop. You'll be safer there. The Security Police don't like me, and they know we've used this as a headquarters. Goodbye now. God take care of you all."

"And you," returned Anyuka.

Teresa couldn't speak. Instead she groped for her mother's hand and held it tight.

Chapter Two

Twilight was beginning to fall as Teresa cautiously opened the door of her mother's little shop and looked up and down the street. She had been out more than once that afternoon, in spite of the Russian tanks that rumbled past on their way to the square still held by a little army of Freedom Fighters.

Last week, when for five glorious days they had thought Hungary was free, seemed a long time ago. Even the fighting was different now from what it had been in those first five days of the revolt. Then, when she had mingled with the crowds, when she had listened to Janos and his friends, she knew they were fighting with hope; now they were fighting with desperation.

Ammunition and supplies were running low. You couldn't fight tanks and guns with bare hands. Every day, every hour, many Freedom Fighters were lost.

Somewhere out there with that gallant band were Janos

and their cousin, Stephan, and Ferenc, and Teresa suspected that Belo had joined them. He knew how to handle a rifle with the best of them. The Communist party had seen to that—the party they had now risen against.

Now that her arm was almost healed, Teresa longed to be out fighting with the others. Plenty of fourteen-year-old girls were doing just that, in the square, on the street, on roofs of buildings. Her friend Piroska Zelk was one of them. But Janos said she could be of more use collecting food and other needed articles—bottles to hold the gasoline they threw at the tanks, shoelaces to use for wicks, and gasoline, if she could find any.

She had two large loaves of bread now and some cheese, and better than that, a little bundle of shoelaces from the shop of Bacsi Zelk, Piroska's uncle. She had a few bottles too, collected wherever she could find them. These precious items must not fall into the hands of the Russians. *I mustn't either,* Teresa thought.

If only she had someone to watch with her—to help a little! But Anyuka had gone to work in the hospital where Zita was a student nurse. Her brother, Belo, she had not seen since noon.

She hesitated in the doorway, uncertain how best to proceed. There was no safe way, she knew that, but some ways and times were more dangerous than others. As she stood listening intently, she heard hasty, almost furtive, footsteps coming toward her from around the rear of the shop. With a quick, terrified movement, she closed and bolted the door.

But now someone was there—someone who knocked urgently yet not loudly. Surely no enemy would knock like that. "Teresa! Teresa!" a familiar voice called softly. "Open! Quick!"

Why, that was Ferenc! Teresa had the door open in a flash, and Ferenc stepped quickly inside, his white face strained but determined, dark eyes sunken a little from lack of sleep, but nevertheless alert. Teresa felt a wave of relief rushing over her. Ferenc would know what to do.

"Oh, Ferenc!" she exclaimed. "I'm so glad you've come. I've collected things to take, but I don't know where to take them or which way to go or where they're needed most or—"

Ferenc stood looking down at her, his face somber. "I know where Janos is, and Stephan, and some of the others. That is, I know where they *were*."

"*Were*?" Teresa half whispered.

Ferenc hesitated. Until lately he had thought of Teresa as not much more than a little girl, a mimic who could always make them laugh, fond of games and full of fun. Now she seemed suddenly to have grown up, and her eyes were steady and serious as she waited for his answer.

"They're up on the roofs, Teresa, fighting enemy tanks. It's—it's terribly dangerous. You know what they do—watch till the tanks are right underneath and then throw hand grenades and bottles of gasoline fired with shoelace wicks into them. Some of our fellows have Tommy guns. They've wrecked a lot of tanks, but they get shot at with machine guns." He paused. "Polgar Huba was killed—I saw him—and his brother Josef wounded. Your cousin Stephan," he added hesitatingly, "well, he was wounded, but I think—I hope—not too seriously. None of them have eaten—all day."

"I have some food and shoelaces and bottles," said Teresa eagerly. "If we can just get them to the boys."

"Good! I have a siphon, and I know where we can get some gasoline out of a wrecked tank. Janos said he left some cans here—in the back room—and some hand grenades packed in wrappings your mother had here."

"Yes, I know," said Teresa, leading the way quickly to where a few innocent-looking packages, holding deadly materials, were concealed. "And here are the cans. We can put the bread and things in the cans and carry more that way. But how will we get there, Ferenc?"

Her voice was anxious. Ferenc looked at her doubtfully. "Maybe I'd better go alone," he said.

"No! Two can carry more."

"And there'll be two chances to get there instead of one," said Ferenc quietly. "You understand, Teresa, there's a chance we may not get there at all."

"I know. I went out more than once today—had to watch my chance and then do a lot of dodging to get these things." She was pulling on her coat as she spoke, slipping a flashlight into her pocket.

"Come on then; let's get started. We'd better go a roundabout way I know, back of the shop. If we're able to get over a couple of streets, it will be a little easier. Then we can go partway underground. You know when the Germans were here, they made doors in the basements to get from building to building during air raids. They were bricked up after the war, but we've opened some. It helps."

But even as he raised his hand to lift the bolt, Teresa gave his arm a jerk. "Wait!" she whispered. "There's another one coming—another tank." Her face was white, her eyes big as she looked up at Ferenc.

Past the little shop, on down the street, rumbled the tank, and as they stood listening, silent and tense, there came the sound of an explosion.

"We got that one," said Ferenc grimly.

"But oh, Ferenc, there are so many—so many, and not very many of us."

"No, but one thing," said Ferenc, "they taught us how to fight tanks. Think of that, they taught it in a course at the university, and Janos and my brother Artur and the other fellows learned well! They thought they were 'indoctrinating' us." His voice was full of scorn. "They didn't know they were teaching us to fight them. And the boys have added a few things that weren't in the course. You know Artur is a whiz in chemistry. Well, coast is clear now, I guess."

"Ferenc, let's try getting out of the window at the back. It's quite high, but I think it would be better than the street door. Even though it's getting toward dusk, two of us, with these cans and things, would be pretty noticeable on the street. It isn't like when I was out alone this afternoon with no bigger bundles than bread."

"Good idea!" agreed Ferenc, a little surprised. He was sure Teresa was frightened, yet in spite of it, she was capable of quick, clear thinking. "If we can get over a couple of streets, I think we'll make it to their hideout."

Ferenc managed the high window without much trouble. The difficulty came in getting out the cans and the packages of grenades. At every sound of a footstep or tank, Ferenc dropped to the ground close beside the shop while Teresa waited inside, wondering anxiously if they would ever get started.

The packages were almost all out when there came a loud knock and rattling at the front door. A rough voice shouted, "Open here! Open, I say!" Teresa, not daring to wait another moment, pulled herself up to the windowsill, dropped to the ground, gathered her precious bundles, and silently followed Ferenc.

Anxious to get away from the vicinity of the shop as quickly as possible, yet keenly aware of the need for caution, he made his way past houses, in the shelter of stone walls, taking every possible advantage of gaps and rubble left by the fighting.

Both were sure they had narrowly escaped being taken by the A.V.H., the dreaded Security Police, but neither of them spoke a word. Indeed, it required every shred of concentrated effort to make headway. Sometimes they had to walk in a crouching position with their heavy loads, and often they had to stop to look this way and that or just to listen. Tanks rumbled along the next street, machine-gun shots whined nearby. At any sound of danger, they flattened themselves against a building or hid as well as they could in some ruin, eyes and ears alert. Teresa hoped her companion could not hear the pounding of her heart.

But at last they turned into a street where Ferenc, pausing for one last cautious look, darted through a half-wrecked doorway and down a steep stairway, Teresa close behind him.

He stopped in the basement of a partially ruined building, putting down his load for a moment and motioning Teresa to do the same. "The rest of the way is pretty safe—underground through basement rooms and passages. Teresa, it's a good thing you thought of going out that back window. The police would have gotten us if we'd gone that front way. They probably broke into the shop when you didn't answer."

"They got fooled, and it isn't the first time," said Teresa.

"Nor the last," returned Ferenc. "Now, Teresa, I want you to wait here while I go out and siphon off some gasoline. It isn't far, and we're going to need it tonight. You aren't afraid to stay alone, are you?"

"Of course not!" said Teresa.

Ferenc started away, then turned back. "If—if it takes too long," he said, "you go straight ahead—through that door and right on—and you'll find the boys' hideout. It's about six houses down."

Teresa only nodded, but her heart beat fast as she waited there alone. Not even Ferenc knew for sure that Janos and the others were in the hideout, and certainly no one could be sure that Ferenc would return safely.

But to her great relief, he was back almost before she had expected him, his face triumphant. "I got a couple of cans full," he said. "Now, come on. We haven't very much farther to go—I hope."

In the ruined basement of a building where walls leaned crazily to form a strange kind of shelter, they found Ferenc's brother Artur, Cousin Stephan, who had a bandage around his head, a young man whom Teresa did not know, and, most welcome of all to Teresa's eyes, her brother Janos.

She took one look at the white, unshaven faces and rushed to her brother. "Oh, Janos," she said, her voice shaking, "you're all right!" Then she steadied herself with an effort and said, "We've brought food."

"Good! We haven't eaten since yesterday," said Janos quietly, but it seemed to Teresa his dark eyes lost some of their weariness. All four crowded around while she rapidly tore the bread and cheese into pieces and handed them out.

"Bottles and shoelaces, I see. We're sure glad to get those," said Artur, as they ate hungrily. "How about gas? Got some?"

"Two cans," said Ferenc proudly.

"Good boy!" said Janos. "Just what we need."

"Cousin Stephan, should you be here?" Teresa asked anxiously.

"Where else?" Stephan asked. "They haven't knocked me out yet."

"Janos, do you know where Belo is?" she asked next. "I haven't seen him for hours, and I'm worried."

"Oh, I know where he is all right." In spite of the tension, weariness, and danger, a little smile broke out on Janos' face. "That kid! Twelve years old! Somehow, in the face of tanks and soldiers and police and fighting, he scouted around and found us. He's keeping watch out there for us now. And Budapest is full of kids like him!" Janos' voice was proud. "Did you have much trouble getting here?"

While the young men ate their hurried meal, Teresa and

Ferenc told of their escape from the shop. In the midst of the story, a boyish voice called out softly, "Panzer!"

Teresa saw weariness drop from that group of young men and excitement and determination take its place as they went swiftly into action. Ferenc and Artur seized bottles and cans of gasoline; Janos and the others picked up boxes of grenades.

The tank was rumbling nearer, but the boys were ahead of it, running swiftly up the stairs to the roof. The next instant, Belo burst into the shelter. "They're almost here! There are two at least—maybe three," he panted.

"Look, I'll take a can of gasoline, and you take some of those bottles. We can fill them for the boys up on the roof," said Teresa.

Belo's eyes blazed with eagerness. "They haven't let me up on the roof before," he said. "Janos wouldn't want you up there either, but—"

Teresa was scarcely listening. "We can help," she said and fairly flew up the stairs, Belo at her heels, to the roof where the little band was rapidly making ready for the attack on the tank.

No one was talking. There was no necessity. They had done this before. Teresa was amazed at the speed and precision with which they worked. Ferenc and Artur filled bottles with gasoline. Stephan put in shoelace wicks. Janos tore open a package of grenades and fitted two or three together. The other young man kept watch.

"Now!" Janos said softly. Ferenc and Artur and Stephan lighted wicks and tossed the bottles over the roof and outward; the grenades quickly followed.

There was a loud explosion, and Janos said grimly, "We got that one. Exploded right on it."

"That tank won't roll again—just block up the street for the next," said Ferenc with satisfaction.

Teresa, filling a bottle, found her hands trembling, so she

spilled more than she got in, but she managed to fill it and thrust in a wick.

Then Ferenc noticed her. "You here!" he exclaimed. "You must go—"

"Everybody must go!" commanded Janos. He seized Teresa's bottle and lighted and threw it just as machine gun fire began to take the roof. "Quick!" He dropped flat, jerking Teresa down beside him, and squirmed toward the opening, the others following.

"We must get to a different shelter—fast," he directed, as they raced down the stairs. He wasted no words and made the most sparing use of his flashlight; quickly he led them single file through underground rooms and passages to a spot where he felt they might be safe for time enough to plan further action.

"Whew, that was fast!" breathed Teresa, trying to make out her companions in the dim light which filtered in from the street through the high, small windows.

"We weren't a minute too soon," said Artur, for they could hear machine-gun fire still going on.

Janos was looking anxiously around. "We weren't soon enough," he said in a low voice. "Stephan isn't here—and Zoltan. I thought they were right with us."

He was peering down the passage, flashing his light, looking and listening; then without a word, he started back.

"Janos!" cried Teresa. "Where are you going?"

"I'm going to find them," he answered.

"Oh, but you can't! The machine guns! The soldiers and everything! They'll be looking for you!"

Artur and Ferenc started up. "We're going too!"

"No! Be crazy for us all to go. There may be a chance to do more fighting. You better wait for that. There's still some stuff to fight with."

"One of us at least must go with you," said Artur firmly. "I'm going. You may need help with the boys," he added in a low tone.

"Come on then. Ferenc, you know the fighting procedure. You can take over if you have to. Wait here for us till the street is quiet. It may take us a while. If we aren't back in a reasonable time, and it seems clear enough, try to get home. Better not go back to the shop. Go to the flat. We'll come home as soon as we can."

No one wanted to be left behind, Ferenc least of all. But he had learned in those few days to obey orders without question, and Janos, he knew, had good judgment as well as courage. He had been in the fighting and could clearly picture the danger Janos and his brother faced in going back.

Teresa and Belo knew well enough that the two might not return, and their hearts were heavy as they listened to the footfalls going down the stony passage.

Chapter Three

THE THREE WAITING in the dark hideout listened anxiously for any sound that would tell them Janos and Artur were returning with the two they had gone to seek. Now and then a slight noise in the passage or adjoining rooms made them start up hopefully. But as they strained to listen, they could tell it was only some little shower of loosened brick or stone falling.

Outside there were sounds enough—machine-gun fire, shouts, brusque orders, rifle shots, tanks crunching up. "They can't get by the one we wrecked," said Ferenc. "We foxed them that much, anyway—got the street blocked."

"Sounds as if they're trying to move that tank," said Belo, who had had his own share of experience in the fighting. "And that will take some doing."

"I can't stay here much longer," Ferenc said restlessly. "I want to get out and help."

Teresa crouched in the darkness without saying much.

The terrible scene on the roof kept going through her mind, and her lively imagination pictured Janos and Artur up there trying, in the midst of machine-gun fire, to rescue the two left behind, trying in the thick of fighting to get them to some place of safety. If they would only come!

She feared too for the safety of her mother and thought of the little shop, wondering if it had been ransacked and wrecked after she and Ferenc left it.

In spite of herself, she shivered. But then she thought of her mother's dark eyes, so full of fire, and took courage from the thought. Anyuka was working for freedom with as fierce a determination as her sons. If ever she felt frightened, she certainly didn't show it.

Some of the hospitals had been shelled, Teresa knew, and she fervently hoped that Anyuka and Zita would be home when she and Ferenc and Belo got there—if they succeeded in getting there at all.

Teresa didn't know how long they waited there, but at last the street outside was comparatively quiet—they could hear shooting only in the distance.

"It shouldn't take the boys so long, should it, Ferenc?" she whispered at last.

"Maybe the way back is blocked with fallen stone or something. They must have—they must have taken Stephan and Zoltan some other way," Ferenc answered hesitatingly.

"It must be toward morning, Teresa," Belo said. "We'd better try to make it home, the way Janos said."

Teresa didn't see how she could bear to go out on the street again. The refuge seemed safe and quiet in comparison. But those were Janos' orders, and if her twelve-year-old brother could do it, she certainly should be able to. And she was so very anxious to find Anyuka. If only Janos were there to lead the way! But Ferenc had done a good job of getting them there. She'd have to trust him to get them back.

Ferenc was plainly relieved to be doing something active. "Lend me your flashlight, Teresa," he said and led the way down the passage where Janos and Artur had gone. He wanted to get to the roof and see if the boys had reached it and gotten away. "Whew!" he said softly, flashing his light around. "Plenty of bricks and stone came down with all that shelling. We'll have to climb over some of those heaps."

"They never could have got Stephan and Zoltan out this way," said Teresa. "Oh, I hope they weren't trying it when these things fell."

The same thought had occurred to Ferenc, and he went slowly, using his flashlight often. All three kept rigid watch, but they saw no sign of anyone as they made their painfully slow way along passages and through basements. Finally, they came to the room with the stairway leading to the roof.

Here Ferenc paused. "You two wait here," he said. "I'm going up."

"Me too!" said Belo. Ferenc, knowing that he might need help, nodded.

Teresa, her mind full of both hope and dread, started after them. But Ferenc said, "Teresa, you stay here. The less moving around there is up there, the better. We'll let you know if we need you."

They were down again in a few minutes. "No one up there. No sign of anything but the fighting," Ferenc said, his face very sober.

"Where do you suppose they are?" Teresa whispered, hardly able to form the words.

"I don't know," was all Ferenc could say. "Come now, let's hurry. We'll go right on and see if we can get out another way."

Flashing his light often now, he led the way through still

more underground passages, and at last he paused. "Yes, there's a stairway—see!" he exclaimed in a low voice. Up the stairs they went, to a battered street door. Here Ferenc paused again, looking cautiously out into the street and in all directions. "Looks fairly clear," he said. "Now, be sure we all stick together."

Teresa felt more frightened this time than when they had come. Then her determination to help Janos and the others had buoyed her up, and the one thought had been to get the things they needed to him and the other boys. Now she got courage from the thought that they might find Janos and Artur and the others at home, and she whispered it to Ferenc.

"We can only hope," he answered, and then, moved by the anxiety in her voice, added reassuringly, "I've seen those fellows get out of some pretty tight places these last few days. Now come on; I don't think this is going to be as hard as coming over was."

Ferenc was right. There was much more wreckage than when they had come, and here there were tanks and debris blocking their way, but they had no heavy packages to carry this time. Such fighting as was still going on had moved to other parts, and there were few people on the streets.

He went cautiously, nevertheless, for his great fear now was falling into the hands of the Security Police. Whenever the three heard any sounds, they promptly hid. At last they came out on the street where Teresa's home was. Her feeling of relief and hope was great as they went up the stairs of the building, for she caught a faint thread of light under the door of their apartment.

She knocked softly—two long and three short knocks—a signal they had arranged during these last dangerous days. A bolt slid quietly back, and the door opened just enough to show Zita standing there. She opened the door quickly and shut it as soon as the three were safely inside.

Teresa took one swift look around the room, and her heart sank. There was no sign of her mother, and it was only then she realized how much she had counted on finding her there. But the next instant, there she was, coming in from the kitchen with a tray of tea things and a large plate of bread and butter.

Teresa rushed to give her mother a hug. "Oh, Anyuka!" she said, and then, to keep herself from bursting out crying, added, "Let me pour the tea."

There was something in the simple, everyday act of pouring tea that Teresa found very steadying. Chilled as she was, the homely old teapot felt warm and comfortable to her hands. As they gathered there, eating and drinking together, a feeling of comradeship and common danger drew them very close.

"Janos—did you see him? Do you know where he is?" asked Zita, and Anyuka too waited anxiously for the answer.

The story of the night's adventures—the fight on the roof, the return trip to rescue Stephan and Zoltan—was soon told. Zita's large gray eyes grew even wider as she listened. When the tale ended, she turned to Anyuka. "We must find them," she said. "Maybe they're hurt—maybe—" she broke off.

"I'll go," said Ferenc, starting up.

"Me too," said Belo eagerly.

But Anyuka shook her head. "We all have taken dangerous chances these last days, and we shall again. But there would be no use whatever in this, and you know what Janos would say to it."

Reluctantly the boys sat down again, knowing that what Anyuka said was true. And even Zita gave a little sad nod.

"But you and Zita," said Teresa, "how did you come to be here together?"

"Our hospital was shelled," said Zita bitterly. "Our work there is finished. The Red Cross and some other helpers managed to get there, and together we got the survivors on their way to safer places, we hope."

In the silence that fell on the little group, cautious footsteps were heard on the stairs. Once again, Zita flew to the door, her face so alive and eager they all knew she could hardly wait for the signal knock before she opened it.

She gave a low, happy cry, quickly muffled as Janos seized her in his arms and held her tight.

"Oh, Zita," they heard him say softly. "I was so afraid—I heard about your hospital—"

"Where are the others?" Ferenc asked, for Artur was the only other one to enter, and he quickly closed and bolted the door.

"That's a story you'll hardly be able to believe," said Janos. "We found the boys on the roof, all right," he said, "but we couldn't get them back the way we'd come—passage was blocked by falling stones. Then we found we could get them out another way. Stephan had been wounded again and Zoltan badly hurt."

"And they actually said we shouldn't have taken the chance of coming back," said Artur. "They said while we were all in one piece, we should keep on fighting or get clear out of this."

"They needed help, and right away," Janos continued, "so we thought we'd try to get them to the hospital where Anyuka and Zita were. But then someone on the street told us that it had been badly shelled. We still had to get the boys someplace. Stephan could just barely walk, with help, but we had to carry Zoltan. It was a slow, hard journey."

"For them especially," said Artur. "We knew there was a Red Cross first aid station not too far away, and we thought if we could get them there, they'd be taken care of. We did get across the street from it. The men in the station saw our plight, and a fellow tried to get over to help us, but then the Russian soldiers popped up from somewhere and started firing.

"The fellow was just winged, but of course he had to give up trying to help, and we didn't know how we were going to get the boys over. They finally managed to throw a rope across the street. We fastened that under Stephan's arms and wrapped our coats around him to give some more protection, and they pulled him across the street. Then we did the same for Zoltan."

"It was getting toward morning, and there was just enough dim light for us to see," Janos took up the story, "but not enough light for anyone a distance away to see what we were doing. We got the boys safely across where they could get help. They gave them first aid and will get them to some kind of a hospital as soon as they can. The boys are in good hands. They'll be all right, I think."

"And then how about you?" asked Anyuka. "How did you make it here?"

"We're used to that kind of travel," said Janos, and in spite of his weariness, he smiled a little. "Dodging along as fast as we could part of the time, hiding when necessary."

"They're really out for Janos," said Artur. "They know he's been leading a group that's wrecked a lot of tanks."

"Artur's in demand too," said Janos. "We mustn't stay here. They're likely to track us, and all of you will be in danger."

"We're in danger anyway," said Zita quietly. "Now you're here we aren't going to let you out of our sight for this day at least. You've got to get some sleep and some food. You've been fighting night and day, and you've got to have rest. Besides, it's so light now you'd easily be seen."

"Did you hear anything about Piroska, or Mother and Father?" Ferenc asked.

Artur shook his head, his face somber. "Not a word. You know Piroska—how daring she is. Too many things have happened. I saw Bacsi today." This was good news, for everyone liked the Zelks' great uncle.

"Maybe he'll get some word of Piroska," said Teresa hopefully.

In Ferenc's mind a resolution was forming to find out somehow about his mother and father and sister. He was anxious especially about his mother, only now recovering from a serious illness. It seemed very long since he had seen any of them, though it was only a few days. How he wished his mother were out of the country.

He was about to speak of it when Anyuka said hesitatingly, "I've been thinking, seriously, that we mustn't stay here—any of us. Much as I hate to say it, the best thing we can do now is to get out of Budapest, all of us—get out of Hungary."

Janos sprang up, his eyes full of fire. "Not while there's a Russian tank we can wreck," he said.

But Artur said, "Your mother may be right, Janos. We had twelve fellows in our group yesterday. Now you and I are the only ones left to fight. And they're after us."

"I suppose you know," said Ferenc, "that they're rounding up young Freedom Fighters—sending off freight loads to labor camps. We wouldn't be much use to Hungary there."

"Oh, Janos," burst out Teresa, "you wouldn't do any good being killed here or shipped away. And you're so strong and so—well, you always seem to know what to do. You could help get people across the border."

Janos looked at Zita, but she didn't speak. He knew that whatever he decided, she would stand by him. This was one time he didn't know what was best to do. It was a terrible decision to have to make.

But even as he stood silent, they all looked at each other apprehensively. Once again there were footsteps on the stairs, followed by a knock on the door. And this time it was not the familiar signal.

Chapter Four

NO ONE MADE a move toward the door, and the eyes fixed upon it were filled with dread. Then came another knock, and a low voice said urgently, "Is anyone there? It's I, Bacsi."

Ferenc made one leap for the door, opened it, drew his uncle inside, and shut and bolted the door.

For a moment Bacsi stood leaning against a table, his breath coming fast. "I was afraid I was caught one time there, but I got inside a building just in time, and they didn't see me come here, I'm quite sure. The Security Police may not care for old fellows like me, but they know what you young folks have been doing, and they might think I could lead them to you." Short and stocky, with keen light-brown eyes and grizzled hair, Bacsi looked as if he might be capable of making plenty of trouble himself for the Security Police.

"Mother and Father and Piroska? Do you know where they are?" Anxious questions burst from Artur and Ferenc.

To the relief of both lads, Bacsi replied, "Your mother and father, I hope, are safely over the border into Austria by now." Then he hesitated. "Your house, I must tell you, was badly shelled. It's a shambles. There was no place there for your mother."

"But how did they get away?" asked Anyuka.

"By train. It was standing in the station, and the railroad men, you know, are sympathetic to the patriots."

"What about tickets?"

"You don't need tickets. They simply let the train fill up and then just roll out of the station. Folks are able to get a good distance that way, but the rest of the journey must be on foot. It won't be easy, but your mother and father can do it, I think. There were other neighbors in the group."

"Why didn't you go along?" asked Ferenc.

Bacsi grinned, almost sheepishly, and that grin bringing out the familiar twinkle and the well-used laugh wrinkles around his eyes somehow made them all feel better. "Well, to tell the truth, I did go most of the way—far enough so I felt pretty sure of their safety. I wasn't too sure at first your mother could make it, but now I'm hopeful that she did."

"I thought that was about the size of it," said Ferenc. "And now, why did you come back? You were a good way toward the border, I take it."

"Well, yes. So I learned the ropes a little. It isn't an easy trip, I can tell you that, and you can't always count on those trains either. I thought I might be able to help the rest of you, and maybe some others, over the border. It's about all an old fellow like me is good for." He spoke lightly and hurried on before anyone could comment. "Some of the way you can go through forest, but there's open country too, and you never know where soldiers will be posted. They might be almost anywhere."

"They'll certainly be along the border," said Janos.

"Piroska—was she with them?" asked Teresa anxiously.

Bacsi hesitated again. "Piroska I haven't seen for some time," he said, and there was no smile in his eyes now. "The last I saw her, she had a rifle over her shoulder."

"We've got to find her," said Ferenc with a kind of desperate earnestness.

"Yes. I have been trying tonight," said his uncle. "But the Fighters are scattered in many places. Piroska is brave and resourceful, and she is with others like herself. We will do our best to find her, but it may not be possible."

"We couldn't leave without her," said Artur firmly.

This nephew was proving to be something of a surprise, Bacsi thought. He had always been the quiet, studious member of the family, but now in this crisis he was, if not so much of a leader, at least as staunch a fighter as Janos, who had always been high-spirited and fearless. A crisis brought out the worst or the best in people. In this group, Bacsi thought proudly, it had brought out the best.

Together they talked, trying to make a workable plan. Ideas were suggested, considered, rejected, new ones brought forward. Anyuka and the girls made fresh tea, got out bread and cheese and sausage. Janos was most reluctant to leave Budapest. Artur and Ferenc felt they could not leave until they had found their sister.

"Bacsi," said Teresa at last, "wouldn't we be more useful across the border, spreading word of what's going on here—maybe getting help for those who stay—than we could be staying here?"

"I am sure of that," Bacsi replied.

"It wouldn't be much use for the boys to be taken prisoner and shipped away, would it?" she said, her eyes on Janos.

"None at all," said Bacsi decidedly. Teresa was a surprise to him too. This didn't sound much like the gay, lighthearted youngster who had always been a special pet of his. This sounded like a clear-thinking, sensible young woman. "Also, the boys especially could help a lot in getting folks out."

"Nurses would be useful too, I suppose," said Zita.

Anyuka nodded, but her eyes were on the boys. She could understand their objections, but she felt that there was little more even valiant fighters like these could do in Budapest, and they might be captured at any time. The Security Police would certainly have these boys high on their list. She was convinced they could be of more use across the border than they would be here. As for Piroska, she was with others of her own courageous, resourceful kind. They might even now be well out of the city. Anyuka said these things quietly, and she could see that her words carried weight.

"We couldn't start now, anyway," said Janos. "Too light. And we're dead on our feet. We'd better get some sleep. Better not take anything off, though, but our shoes. May have to make a quick getaway."

With the help of Zita and Teresa, Anyuka made beds of some sort for all of them. She expected to stay awake herself and make definite plans. But soon the others were asleep, and at last, completely worn out, she too fell into a heavy slumber.

It was Teresa who sat up, suddenly wide awake, her heart pounding. A loud knock had come at the door—a knock like the last one she had heard at the shop door. In an instant she was up and slipping quietly into the room where Bacsi and the boys were asleep. Quickly she shook her brother awake. "Janos!" she said in an urgent whisper. "They're here! The police! Get down the back stairs and into the basement."

By this time the pounding had aroused everybody. Even Belo, usually so hard to wake, was on his feet. The boys and Bacsi seized coats and shoes and swiftly and silently disappeared down the back way.

Teresa looked after them anxiously. In the sub-basement, she knew there was an underground room, built for concealment during the war. If the boys could reach that, they should be safe, for the time, but she was far from sure they could reach it. Guards might intercept them on the way. Anyuka and Zita were wide awake now too, hastily putting on their shoes, straightening their clothing.

"Open that door and quick, or we'll break it down!" came the harsh command. "We know who's in there. No use trying to hide. Open here!"

Anyuka, her face very white, was starting toward the door, while Zita darted into the next room with the whispered words, "Try to give me time to get the sleeping things out of sight!"

"Let me go to the door," Teresa whispered. "They won't expect a kid like me to know as much as they would you."

"Good! I'll help Zita. Keep them out as long as you can."

Teresa was trembling, but some sort of a plan was forming in her mind. Glad for once not to be very big for her age, she quickly tousled her hair in a way that made her look much younger than her fourteen years and managed a big yawn. "Just a minute," she called out in a small, sleepy voice. "I have to get something on." She slipped one foot into her shoe and said, on another yawn, "I'll be right there."

"These Hungarian kids!" she heard a voice storm. "They're the worst! I can deal with grown-ups a lot better."

"Hurry up, there!" shouted another.

Teresa took time to see that Anyuka and Zita were rapidly getting things out of the way. She had always had a gift for acting, but she wasn't thinking of that as she went unwillingly toward the door. She only knew that by whatever means she could, she must keep those officers out as long as possible.

"What is it you want?" she asked sleepily. "Nobody's here."

"No use lying! We know some of the fighters are in there. We want them!"

"They aren't here," said Teresa, moving the doorknob a little. She couldn't keep her voice from trembling, but even then she realized that it was probably a good thing. If she were too calm, they might be all the more suspicious.

The best she could do now was to try to delay the men a little more after the door was open. As she pushed the bolt, it seemed to her that her heart was banging against her ribs so hard everyone must hear it.

Wide awake and frightened as she was, it was hard to get out another yawn, but somehow she managed it. And instead of opening the door just a crack, as she longed to do, she opened it wide. They'd get in anyway, and she was determined not to act afraid and not to let them know that anyone was in hiding.

"You might as well tell us where they are. We're going to search the place anyway," said the first officer, striding in.

Teresa knew very well they would do just that, no matter how she tried to keep them out, so she said, "Very well. You won't find any fighters here."

She sounded so convincing and offered so little resistance that the men hesitated, looking at each other. For a moment she thought they were going away.

But then the first officer said, "We'd better search. These kids can be awfully tricky. We've found that out."

To Teresa's relief, Anyuka and Zita came in now. Their work was finished then, and the search would reveal nothing. Nothing, that is, unless the men went down the back way, and even then, the boys by now must have had a chance to get safely into hiding.

The officers were plainly baffled when their swift but thorough search revealed nothing. "I was sure—" one of them said.

"I *am* sure. I know someone came in here," said the other. "I'm going to keep a sharp eye on this place."

"The way they dodge around, they drive you crazy," said the first. He turned to Anyuka and said angrily, "Is there a back way?"

Without a word she pointed to the kitchen, and the next moment the two men were rushing down the back stairs.

"They're making enough noise. The boys will surely hear them," said Zita, but the three faces were very white. Anyuka's lips were moving silently, and Teresa knew she was praying.

Far below them, at last, a door banged, and Teresa, darting to the window, saw the officers crossing the street. "They didn't find them!" she cried. "They're going away!"

Anyuka dropped into a chair and covered her face with her hands. Zita just stood there, looking thoughtful and resolute. "Tonight is the time we must start," she said quietly. "There is no use waiting—no doubt now we can all be of more service over the border than here."

Anyuka stood up, smoothed back her dark hair with both hands in a way she often did before she went at a big task, and she said, "I am glad to hear you say that, Zita. I'm convinced of it. Now we must decide what to take with us and the best way to carry it, and then get everything ready."

"I'll go just as I am," said Zita. "Everything I had was in my room near the hospital, and there's not much left of that." She paused a moment. "For once I'm almost glad I'm an orphan. At least I have no family of my own to worry about."

"You belong to our family now," said Anyuka gently, "and we'll find whatever you need right here." And because tears were very near the surface with her, and she was sure with the girls also, she said briskly, "Now let's begin to get things ready. We must each take a bundle, and before we go we will put on all the extra clothing we can."

"How about food for the journey? And shouldn't we take some now to the boys?" asked Teresa.

"Pretty soon it should be fairly safe to go down into our own basement," said Anyuka. "And we must try to get out to find food for the journey—more bread and cheese and sausage if we can get it, something good and solid. Food is scarce, we know, since the Russians stopped trucks coming in. But we must try to get some. The journey may take longer than we think."

All of them were thankful to have their hands busy. Teresa offered to scout for the food supplies. "They're afraid of kids like me. Didn't you hear them say so?" she asked with a flash of her old humor. "They said they could manage the grown-ups better."

"And I'll take food down to the basement and talk things over with the boys," said Zita.

Teresa had another object in mind as she set out. She wanted to get some word of Piroska, if possible. On the street or in a shop, there might be someone who knew of her.

At the bakeshop the counters were bare, but the owner knew Teresa. "For our friends I find something," she said and brought out two precious loaves. But she shook her head at Teresa's inquiry. "Piroska Zelk? No, I'm sorry. I haven't heard a word of her."

Teresa met two or three friends as she hurried along the streets, but none of them had seen Piroska, and in spite of her good fortune in finding the bread, she couldn't help feeling downhearted when she turned into the little shop where she hoped to get cheese.

There was no cheese to be had, but she got something she valued much more—a little hopeful news of her friend. "Piroska Zelk?" the proprietor said and stopped to think. "Yes, yes. I heard she was with a group starting for the border. Who was with her, I do not know. Her folks, maybe?"

"Not her folks," said Teresa. "I'm sure of that. Is that all you know?"

"That is all I know. I'm sorry."

Teresa thanked him and hurried out. It was something at least.

The butcher shop, too, looked bare when she went in, but the butcher, who knew the family well, somehow found a large sausage and a smaller one. "Some of our lads hijacked a food truck and got some of it to where they knew it would be put to good use," he said, "for just such folks as you."

To her joy, he also had a little more news of Piroska. "Yes, she went, I am sure. She was with a group of fighters who did the Russians plenty of harm before they ran out of ammunition. Old Gyula Ther was with them. He's all right. He'll get them through."

"Thank you, thank you!" said Teresa. She set off at a rapid pace, anxious to get home with her precious packages and her news of Piroska. That would certainly help Artur and Ferenc make their decision to go. So far she had accomplished even more than she had dared to hope for.

Glad that darkness was gathering as she hurried on, she watched and listened carefully, nevertheless. It would never do to let herself be caught now. Just about this time last night, she and Ferenc had set out on their dangerous mission. How much had happened since then! But now it looked as if things might be clearing a little. If Janos felt he could be of more use going than staying, he would do it.

She had almost reached home when the words of one of the police flashed into her mind, "We'll keep a sharp eye on this place, all right." Hardly realizing what she was doing, she broke into a run. One good spurt, and she'd be there!

But then someone stepped out of a doorway, and a man's heavy hand seized her shoulder.

Chapter Five

For one terrified instant, Teresa stood in full sight of her home, knowing that she might never see any of her family again, might indeed be shipped away on one of those dreaded freight trains.

"Turn around there! Get moving!" said the man harshly.

Teresa forced herself to turn, though her knees were trembling so she could hardly move. But she didn't move fast enough to suit him and received a push that sent her sprawling.

How it happened she couldn't tell, for she heard no one come, but the next instant there were sounds of a struggle behind her. Getting to her feet and turning swiftly, she saw Janos, knife in one hand, the other around her captor's neck. The Russian, his head bent back, was gasping for breath, his arms flailing in the air.

"Quick!" Janos ordered. "Take his revolver out of his holster! Take his ammunition!"

Terrified and trembling though she was, Teresa, nevertheless, obeyed orders.

"Give me the gun," directed Janos. He held it against the soldier, releasing his hold on him. "Now, march!" he said.

"You can't do this! I'm an officer!" burst out the Russian, his breath still coming unevenly.

"We're doing it," said Janos contemptuously. "We'll keep you out of circulation for a while." And a prod from the revolver started the man moving.

Teresa stood holding her breath, watching her brother. "Take your packages and go ahead," Janos said. "Get the boys. They're upstairs—helping. We'll just tie this character up safe in the basement for a while."

Teresa flew up to the apartment, and Artur and Ferenc were immediately dispatched to Janos' aid.

"We didn't even know he'd gone. Thought he was in the kitchen!" exclaimed Ferenc. He and Artur raced down the stairs.

Anyuka and Zita, busy with preparations for leaving, listened in wonder and alarm at her story.

"It's time we were going—high time," said Zita. "Our usefulness here is over."

"We really are going then?" asked Teresa. "When?"

"Tonight," answered her mother, almost in a whisper, as if it was hard to bring out the word.

Even as she spoke, the three boys came in, and Teresa rushed to her brother. "Oh, Janos, you were wonderful! How did you do it? I didn't even hear you come up!" she cried.

"I was watching for you from the window and got down there in a hurry. Came up behind you. The Russians taught us a lot about this kind of fighting. They didn't know how handy it would come in for us."

"Good thing we've got him stashed away there," said Ferenc. "He'd have spread the alarm and most likely none of us would have gotten away tonight—or any other time."

"You are going too, Janos?" Teresa asked.

Janos' face was sober, even sad. "Yes," he said. "We're just about out of ammunition, Teresa. Just a few hand grenades left and a couple of revolvers and maybe enough shells for the journey. Good thing we got the fellow's—that's one extra; we can make use of it and his ammunition too. Not much more we can do here. But we can help folks get over the border, I hope, and once there we can speak the word of how things are here—let the world know—and maybe get some help for the ones remaining."

Teresa nodded. She knew the decision had not been an easy one for him, but once he had made it, he would do everything possible to get his own group over that stretch of ground that lay between them and the border and to help others as well.

She felt both relieved and anxious. At least they were going to make a dash for safety, but she realized there were many dangers on the way to the border and that not everyone who tried had reached it safely.

"Artur and I can't leave without knowing about Piroska," said Ferenc. Teresa was thankful that she could give them hopeful news of their sister.

"Once we're in Austria then, we'll have a good chance of finding her," said Artur. "So I'd say the sooner we get started, all of us, the better." And with this everyone agreed.

The big question was, what would be the best way to start? Many plans had been discussed, and one fact stood out. Much as they longed to keep together when they started off, any such attempt would be foolhardy.

"That would just be asking for trouble," Janos said. "Even in the dark of night, they'd be almost sure to spot us, especially if they have an eye out for us."

"And that they certainly have—for you boys at least," said Zita.

Janos knew that this was true enough, and now he quietly took charge. "The best way is for you folks to go down to the station and take a train, the way Bacsi and the Zelks did."

"Are you sure, Bacsi, there are no guards there?" Anyuka asked, almost as if she couldn't believe it.

"There weren't today. I made it my business to find out. Everything is so disorganized, they apparently haven't even tried to station guards there. It would be quite a job. All the workers in the station itself and the train crews are with the Freedom Fighters. I guess the Russians have their hands full enough as it is."

"Did the folks take anything with them, Bacsi?" asked Artur.

"They took a suitcase and so did a lot of other people. But I could see that it was hard to carry, and it's a long walk—twenty miles or more, depending on how straight they can go and how far the train takes them."

"Zita and I have made bundles for each one—they'll be easier to carry. We can swing them over our backs if necessary—maybe cut a stick to help carry them," said Anyuka. "Before we tie them up, each can put in any special thing he wants and is willing to carry."

"Everyone should have a little money at least," said Bacsi. "I went around to my shop where I had some put away. I'll divide that among us. We can fasten some of it inside our clothing for safety."

"Divide that among your family," Anyuka said. "We can manage with what we have. And now here are the bundles." She went to a table and handed a package to each.

"Artur and Ferenc and I have revolvers," said Janos. "We will divide what ammunition we have left. And the men and boys will each take a hunting knife."

"A dressmaker must be provided with sharp scissors," said Anyuka quietly. "Those I shall hope to use in our new life. Zita and Teresa and I will each have a pair with us."

"They may be useful in more ways than one," agreed Bacsi. "Now do you have extra coats? Better put on as much clothing as possible. It will be cold."

Anyuka nodded. She and Zita had made ready all available extra clothing, and it was divided now among the group. Food, too, was carefully parceled out.

Preparations were soon complete, and if Anyuka's eyes were tragic as she looked around her beloved home and treasured possessions, her voice was steady. "We are ready then. We will start off two by two, going by different ways, and all try to get on the same train in the station."

"One minute more," said Bacsi. "I have been thinking of how we might get together again if we should be separated. I have a good old friend on a farm about fifteen miles from the Austrian border, near the village of Ladovar. If we get the right train, it will take us almost that far. In case we get separated, let us make that our objective. We could take shelter there. He would hide us, if necessary. I saw him when I went with our folks, and he told me if I got back that way, he would help any way he could. He is strongly on our side. Even if I were not there, he would help any of you, I am sure. Only we must be discreet and try not to be seen going there, for his sake as well as ours."

Janos nodded, looking somewhat relieved. "I have been thinking that Artur and I, at least, should not try to go by train. We are too likely to be taken and endanger not only ourselves but all of you. We can ride our bicycles and make good time on those. Tell us, Bacsi, just how do we get to this farm?"

Bacsi thought for a moment and took a small notebook and pencil out of his pocket. "I will quickly make a simple map for each," he said. "Keep it hidden with your money."

"When you have one done, let us make copies," said Zita, and the maps were soon finished and handed around.

Bacsi gave careful directions and added bits of information that he thought would be useful. "This farm is not one of the largest, but very neat and with a good house and barn—built together, of course—on a hillside, a great poplar tree out in front. Remember my friend's name, Szalay—Josef Szalay. His wife's name is Mara—good patriots, both."

"We will try to meet you at the end of the train journey, but it's good to know of this place," said Janos. "And now I think we are ready."

Ferenc and Belo longed to go by bicycle too, and said so, but they could see that Janos was right when he told them they might be needed, with Bacsi, to help the women. "We'll do our best to be on hand with the last dangerous lap of the journey," Janos promised. "But they may need help before that."

"What do you think is the best way to start out from here?" Artur asked his uncle.

"We had better go downstairs together and make as sure as we can that all is clear. Then Belo and I start first. I know the ropes a bit and how things are done at the station. Teresa and Ferenc start a few moments later. Then Zita and Anyuka. We each go by a different way."

"Good!" said Janos. "As soon as you all are gone, Artur and I will be on our way. Who knows, we may get to the destination before you do! Maybe we'll be waiting for you when your train stops. Or we might even be milking cows at Szalay's when you get there."

He tried to speak lightly, but in spite of all their efforts, tears were in their eyes when they said goodbye. The Austrian border seemed a long way off. They could not even be sure that they would reach the station in safety.

Fortunately, the distance was not great, and the darkness helped cover their going, though it also forced them to make their way slowly because of rubble and wreckage.

"Oh, Ferenc," Teresa whispered, as they went silently down the dark streets, "we mustn't be taken now."

"We're not going to be," said Ferenc stoutly. Then he jerked her arm quickly and drew her into the shelter of a doorway. Someone was coming. But the footsteps turned at the corner, and again the two were on their way. Once more they had to stop and hide, but at last the station loomed before them.

"Here we are!" said Ferenc on a deep breath of relief. "Now to find the others."

The big station was overflowing with people, and no one seemed to be trying to keep any kind of order. Teresa, looking anxiously about, at first saw no sign of Bacsi and Belo. But then her heart gave a bound, for there they were, elbowing their way through the crowd toward them.

"We've been watching for you. Took longer than we thought, and we were getting anxious," said Bacsi.

"We had to hide a couple of times," explained Ferenc.

"Anyuka and Zita ought to be here soon," said Teresa anxiously.

Bacsi nodded, his eyes scanning the crowd, and the little group stood silently, waiting and hoping.

A train had left not very long ago, someone told them, and now in the big train shed, passengers were filling another. There was no panic. People moved with a certain quiet desperation.

"Oh, I wish they'd come," said Teresa. "What will we do if they don't come?"

"They'll come," said Bacsi quietly, and then, in a voice that plainly showed the relief he felt, "There they are!" And he hurried toward them.

Anyuka's face was very pale, and she held tightly to Bacsi's arm as he led the way to the train.

"Room for six?" he asked the guard.

"Get on," was the reply.

"Come, Belo," said Anyuka, taking the arm of her youngest. "We must be very sure to stay together."

The first three were swept on to the train with the surging crowd, but when the next three tried to board, the guard shook his head and put up his hand as if reluctant to do so. "Every inch filled on that car," he said. "Try farther back."

Through the window, Teresa could see Anyuka pushed unwillingly into a seat, saw her half rise again, her eyes searching the crowd, while Belo and Bacsi too watched anxiously.

"Come on," said Ferenc, but the girls didn't need urging. "This next coach—they're filling that up fast, but you girls can shove in there all right. I'll run ahead down along the train and hop on somehow, even if I have to stand on the last step."

But the next coach was filled up too, and Ferenc had disappeared in the crowd. The girls started to run down the platform, hoping to find a place in the next coach, but already the train was beginning to move.

Teresa stopped running and just stood there. It didn't seem possible the train could go without them, so concentrated had been the efforts of all of them to reach it together.

Up ahead she could see her mother leaning far out of the window, her face frantic. And as the train rolled slowly by, they could see Ferenc clinging to a precarious perch on a step.

With despairing eyes, Teresa watched the train disappearing down the track. "Oh, Zita," she burst out. "Will we find them again? Will the next train go to the same place?"

Brave as Zita had been from the beginning, her voice faltered now. "Teresa," she said, "I don't know."

Chapter Six

Though the girls were full of their own worries, there was plenty of opportunity to help others while they waited for the next train. Teresa and Zita were separated from their own people, it is true, but they at least had hope of finding them again.

Many of the crowd in the station had no such hope. A boy no older than Belo was making his way alone to the border. The grandparents with whom he lived had sent him off as the best thing they could do for him.

A sad-faced young woman with a small baby was making a desperate effort to get to safety. "Her husband was killed in the fighting," an older woman explained in a low voice to the girls. "We will try to help her. The last word he sent was that she and the child must get over the border."

Many children were there, many young and middle-aged people, a few who were elderly. Most of them had a curiously lost, yet resolute expression. Some had been wounded, and these Zita could help to make more comfortable, while Teresa held a sleeping child to give a tired mother a little rest.

It seemed a long time before the next train was ready, but there it was at last. The two girls were well in front this time as the crowd surged toward the train.

Teresa wanted to stop at the coach steps and ask the guard if this train was going to the same place as the last one, but there was not an instant's time. She was carried swiftly along in the rush for the coaches, up the steps, and actually into a seat. She hadn't been able to get a scrap of information, but at least Zita was right behind her. The two made a pact to let nothing divide them, and now they sat crowded together, side by side, trying to take up as little space as possible.

In just a few minutes, the car was packed, every seat crowded, every inch of standing room jammed.

A gentleman who looked as if he might have some information was beside her, and to him Teresa timidly put her question, but he shook his head and smiled a little, his eyes kind and sympathetic. "As to that, it is hard to say. I talked with one of the officials in the station, and he said nothing is on schedule. They are just taking people as far as possible. I hope you will find your folks, but if all landed at the same place, think how difficult it would be to make an escape. Our hope lies in scattering as much as possible—that way we can better avoid being captured and shot or sent back."

There was sense to that, Teresa could see, but she felt both frightened and forlorn, and her eyes sought Zita's for comfort. "What are we going to do when we get to the end of the ride if the folks aren't there?" she whispered.

Zita found her hand and gave it a reassuring squeeze. "We'll just wait and see what the others do," she answered. Both girls were counting more than they admitted to each other on being reunited with their own group at the end of the journey.

The ride was an anxious one for all. No one could be sure if they would reach their destination or even what that destination would be. From time to time, rain fell heavily. But the train went steadily on until it stopped at a small town where the end of the ride was announced.

Passengers streamed off, gathered in small or larger groups, and most of them soon melted away into the darkness.

The two girls stood waiting a few moments, uncertain and anxious. If Bacsi and the others had reached this place, they would undoubtedly be waiting and watching. Belo or Ferenc or both might at any moment dart out of the dusk and lead the girls away to begin the journey that must be taken on foot. By now they would have reconnoitered and found out the best way to start. But no one came.

Not far from them, in the dim light of the train, Zita had noticed an old man, bearded and in weather-beaten cap and coat, who had said a word or two to many groups as they went by.

"That old man seems to know about things around here. I'm going to see if he can tell me anything about that other train," Zita whispered.

"Is it all right, do you think, to talk to a stranger here?" Teresa asked anxiously. "We don't know who he is or—"

Zita didn't feel very safe about it herself, but she had to find out somehow. As she went toward him, her heart lightened, for she saw he too had the little red, white, and green emblem they were all wearing.

She glanced at it and then up at the lined and kindly face, which she could see more clearly as he bent toward her in the dim light. But he shook his head at her question. "No, there hasn't been another train in since yesterday afternoon," he answered. And with this bad news, Zita had to go back to her waiting companion.

"What do we do now?" asked Teresa. In her disappointment and despair, she felt more like sitting down on the platform and bursting into tears than doing anything else, and in spite of her efforts, her question ended on a shrill note of fear.

"There's just one thing we can do," answered Zita. "Get our bearings and start for the Szalays' farm.

"I hope this village of Ladovar is not too terribly far away."

Teresa knew that Zita too must be frightened and uncertain, that it could not be easy for her to keep her voice so steady. With a great effort, she got control of herself and said in a more natural tone, "I heard some of those folks say there is a wood near here. Let's try to find out what direction Ladovar is from here. Maybe it would be better to go through the woods than on the open road."

It was not light enough for Teresa to see the look of approval Zita gave her, but she did feel the comradely pressure on her arm, heard the relief in Zita's voice as she said, "That's the girl! Come on then. Maybe the old man can tell us which way to go. We won't mention any names of people—just the village—tell him we hope we can find our folks there."

But now the man had started to walk rapidly away, and the girls had to run to overtake him. At the sound of their hurried footsteps, he turned and listened to their question. His voice was thoughtful when he answered, "Ladovar—to get there you should go to the right. But soldiers are in that direction, and you'd be in danger of getting shot. That's what I was telling people as they came along—to go to the left."

"But why do you stay? You are a refugee too—I see by your colors," said Zita.

"Yes, but I have no folks of my own to consider. So I have stayed here two days, giving directions, warning folks. Now that it is getting toward morning, I will take refuge in the woods here for the day. But first I will try to give you directions." He stood thinking for a moment and then, as if he had come to a sudden decision, said "I had better start you on your way. We must circle the town to avoid the soldiers. Listen!" All of them stood very still, and the sound of shots came clearly to them from the distance. "See, it is as I said—those who went that way will go no further on their journey. As for us, we will keep to the shelter of the woods."

Convinced now that their guide could be trusted, the girls were only too glad to follow him. The rain that had been falling earlier had stopped, but the woods were wet, and they had to make their way with care.

When dawn broke, they paused to eat a little of their precious black bread and sausage. Then they plodded on, stopping now and then to rest a bit while the old man consulted a compass or went forward to make sure they could go on safely.

It was noon when he halted suddenly, and after looking keenly in all directions, bade the girls wait where they were and set off by himself through the trees.

Almost numb with weariness though the girls were, and thankful for a rest, they couldn't help being alarmed at the abrupt command and the man's long absence. When he returned at last, he had a little air of satisfaction that mystified them.

"You wonder why I was gone so long," he said. "I will show you if you follow me. Come. We are just about out of the woods now. We have circled the immediate danger, but doing so took us considerably out of our way."

He talked rapidly as they walked along, and in a few moments paused and pointed to a little hut among the trees. "Woodchoppers' hut," he said. "That is what I was looking for. I knew there was one somewhere near. It will be a shelter for you, at least."

He went quickly forward, and the girls followed him into the hut. It was small and not very clean, but the four walls gave them a little feeling of safety.

"Now I must let you go the rest of the way yourselves. Today you must rest here—I think it will be safe—safer than any other place I can think of. You must get some sleep—you will need it for the rest of your journey. You are almost staggering now, I can see. And it is starting to rain again.

"I wish I could go with you," the old man said. "But new trainloads will be coming in. I must get back, find out where the worst danger is, and warn people. But now the road to Ladovar is quite direct. I can tell you exactly how to get there; and when you have had some rest, it will seem easier. It will be safer for you in the darkness too, for you go mostly through open country now, with little protection from trees. You have flashlights?"

Both girls nodded and then listened intently as he gave directions. "One thing you must watch for," he warned. "There are some swampy places if you get off the road."

"About how long should it take?" asked Zita.

"You should make it in about four or five hours' walk from here, even at night. I am sure you can do it by yourselves. You seem very sensible and intelligent, both of you."

The girls thanked him for all his help and insisted that he share some food with them before he went. "Maybe we'll see you again in Austria," Teresa said, putting all the courage that she could into her voice. "Seems as if we're old friends now." And though they tried to smile as good wishes and goodbyes were exchanged, the girls' hearts were heavy when the old man disappeared through the woods.

"Well," said Zita, trying to speak cheerfully, "he was right. We must try first of all to get some sleep, Teresa."

"But what if soldiers or police or anyone should come? We're warned they might be almost anywhere between

Budapest and the border," said Teresa. "Shouldn't one of us stay awake and watch?"

"I don't believe we could if we tried," murmured Zita, dropping down on the dirt floor and spreading her coat over her.

Teresa hesitated, feeling she didn't dare shut her eyes until they were in some safer place. But Zita stretched out her arm, saying drowsily, "Come, we'll sleep through the afternoon and start out as soon as it gets dark." Teresa dropped down beside her, spread both coats over them, snuggled close to Zita for warmth and comfort, and soon the two girls, thoroughly worn out, were sound asleep.

Darkness had fallen when they awoke suddenly with a feeling that they had slept longer than they intended. They sat up, clutching their coats about them. "Was that a shot?" Zita whispered, still half dazed from the heavy slumber.

"I—I think so," Teresa answered, her teeth chattering. The next instant another shot sounded, followed by a volley, and now they could hear hurrying feet.

"Quick, let's open the door and hide behind it," whispered Teresa. "If the door's open, they aren't likely to think anyone's hidden here."

"Good thought," Zita answered. The girls crept to the corner and stationed themselves behind the opened door, covering themselves as completely as they could with their coats. As they crouched there, still and tense, the running steps came nearer and paused.

"They went this way; I know it," someone said. "I saw them."

"Aw, let them go. I don't want to run around here all night. What's a couple of Hungarians more or less?" came the answer in a disgusted tone.

"I wouldn't care either. I want to get some sleep myself. But I know one of them was that crazy rebel who did so much damage.

I saw him more than once in Budapest. Colonel wants him."

"There were plenty of those crazy rebels. Which one do you mean?"

Both girls stiffened in terror at the answer. "I mean the one they call Janos Nagy."

Teresa heard Zita catch her breath sharply. She herself could not control her trembling. And the Russians were coming nearer.

"Zita, we've got to get out of here," Teresa whispered. If they had seen Janos in Budapest, they might have seen her with him. They might question her about him. They'd certainly arrest both girls.

"Can't. They might hear us," breathed Zita.

In their desperate need, Teresa remembered how she and Ferenc had escaped from the shop, and looked at the hole at the back of the hut that served as a window. "Window," she whispered, and swiftly they groped their way around the wall to reach it.

It was small, but Teresa, with Zita pushing, managed to force her way through it and then to help pull Zita and the bundles out. They dropped to the ground and lay there trembling, pressing close to the building, trying to muffle their breathing, which came fast and hard.

Teresa groped for Zita's hand and held it tight. They had made their escape just in time, for now the soldiers reached the hut, and a beam of light showed they were flashing their torches into it.

"No one would be here with the door open," one said.

But the more cautious and determined one replied, "You never know. They're tricky. I don't expect to find that Janos Nagy here, but there might be others of the bunch, and we could question them. He must not get over the border."

"See here," the first one said, "it looks like rain, and here we've got a little shelter. It's almost morning; let's wait till daylight. They'll probably hole up someplace, too, if they think we've stopped pursuit. Anyway, I'm dead on my feet, and so are you. I don't think they could possibly get through. There are soldiers posted along these roads. And it's pretty open country, you say."

"You're probably right," the other responded wearily. "But they've already given us the slip more than once, and I don't want them to do it again."

"Well, let's go out and flash our torches around the building and call it a day."

The girls listened in terror, but the other voice said scornfully, "You don't think anyone as crafty as Janos Nagy would be hiding around behind a building, do you? He'd do better than that. And if he was there with a revolver, wouldn't we make a fine target, lighted up by our torches?"

"Well, if we aren't going to use torches, we'd better wait till daylight, whatever we do. Anyway, I can't even see straight anymore."

There was a moment's silence. Then to the girls' relief came the answer, "Maybe you're right. Probably the best thing we can do is to get some sleep first."

To Zita and Teresa, lying huddled there in the long, damp grass close to the hut, it seemed an endless wait. But at last heavy breathing told them the soldiers were asleep. Then, without speaking, the two girls began to creep away, putting a good distance between themselves and the hut before either ventured a word.

"Now we have to find Janos," Teresa whispered. "We must warn him that they're looking for him specially."

"Yes," Zita answered, "and we have to be out of here, as far away as we can before daylight, all of us."

But even as she spoke, they saw that dawn was already streaking the sky.

Chapter Seven

"If only we hadn't slept so long!" said Zita, daring to talk more freely when the woodchopper's hut was some distance behind them. "I had hoped we'd still have darkness to cover our journey to Ladovar."

"We must be very careful, but at least we're warned," Teresa answered. "We know there are soldiers somewhere along the way. I just wish we knew where!"

Together the girls paused at the edge of the wood, looking out on the open road that stretched dimly before them in the gay light of early dawn. For the first time in all those dreadful days of fighting and fleeing, they were entirely alone and in strange territory. Teresa felt a desperate longing for her family and Ferenc.

Zita's great longing was for Janos. She felt she had to see him, be sure he was safe. "We must find Janos," she said urgently. "Warn him he's in even more danger than he knows. They don't intend to let him get over the border."

"You know the soldiers said Janos was smart," said Teresa, trying to reassure herself and Zita at the same time. "He'll outwit them."

"But he's so daring. He may take one chance too many," Zita said anxiously. "One thing, I'm sure he wouldn't stay around here. We'd better go along as fast as we can, and we'll keep looking."

"He may even be hiding somewhere along the way and see us. Artur must be with him, so there'd be two of them to watch and help each other." Teresa spoke hopefully, but she didn't feel very brave as they set off together down the road, eating a scanty breakfast as they walked.

It was growing light now, and the girls looked at each tree, hoping that Janos or Artur might step out from behind it or even spring down from its branches. They glanced eagerly at any small building that might have offered the boys shelter, but there was no sign of them.

At first they had the road almost to themselves, but as the morning came on, they began to meet an occasional farm cart or some worker on foot. In each case they gave a greeting which was returned courteously enough, but the looks cast upon them were curious and sometimes suspicious.

Teresa had spent her summers on her grandfather's farm, and now she had a sudden idea. "You know something, Zita? We look too much like city girls. Anyone would notice us. Let's take off our coats and carry them. Anyuka put some warm scarves in our bundles. We can put them on like shawls and tie kerchiefs over our heads."

This was soon done, and both girls were encouraged when the next encounter showed less curiosity and more friendliness. But still they felt far from safe. If they met soldiers who questioned them, it would be a very different matter from meeting these country folk.

"Zita, I'd feel a lot safer if we could go by fields and pastures," said Teresa. "We don't know which of these folks are friends and which ones aren't. That last man stared at us as if he thought we hadn't any business here. He or someone else might carry word to the soldiers."

Zita nodded. "I suppose there are sure to be some Communists here too," she said bitterly, "and they'd inform on us fast enough if they thought we were making for the border."

"Let's get over the fence into that pasture," urged Teresa, and Zita promptly agreed. In another moment the girls were walking along in the pasture, and if they felt uncomfortable and out of place there, at least it seemed safer than the road.

Across the rough ground they went, then through a potato field and into another pasture. Teresa, with her country experience, did not find the going too difficult, and as they went on without being challenged or stopped by anyone, she began to breathe more freely.

But it was a different matter for Zita. Time and again she stumbled over a rock or rough piece of ground, and when they found themselves in a pasture with a herd of cows, she shrank anxiously against the fence. "We can't go through there, Teresa," she said. "We don't know what those cows will do."

Teresa was the strong one this time. She looked at Zita and almost laughed. "You!" she exclaimed. "Why, Zita, the way you worked under shellfire in Budapest. You didn't act a bit afraid of the Russian soldiers. Don't tell me you're afraid of a few cows."

"It's different," returned Zita. "At least the soldiers didn't have horns." Then she straightened suddenly, her eyes alert. "Teresa," she said softly, "did you see something move over by that strawstack?"

Teresa looked quickly, and her heart gave a bound. "It's Janos!" she half whispered.

It was Janos, no question of that. Most of his body was

hidden in the strawstack, but his head was thrust out, and one of his hands gave a slight but jaunty wave.

The girls' first impulse was to rush straight to that strawstack, but the last few days had taught them caution.

"Listen!" whispered Zita. Through the quiet morning air came the dreaded sound of shots. "Must be soldiers not far away."

Once again Teresa's quick thinking and love of playacting came to their aid. "We'll put our coat and bundles under the bushes here," she directed, "and pretend we're in charge of the cows." And at Zita's bewildered look, she said, "Just do the way I do. And if we meet the soldiers, we'll act as unknowledgeable as can be."

A swift glance at the strawstack showed no sign of Janos. He too had taken warning from the shots and had gone into hiding, and the girls were determined that no one should get any information from them.

Now the cows, curious about the intruders in their pasture, gathered about the new milkmaids, staring at them with huge, unwinking eyes, to Zita's great alarm. But Teresa, who had often driven cows at her grandfather's farm, quickly found a stick and began herding them into line.

Then Zita saw something coming over the hill that made her completely forget her fear of cows. "Soldiers!" she whispered in a panic.

Teresa tried to act as if she didn't hear her, but her voice trembled as she said, "Time for the cows to be milked," and started driving them toward the barnyard some distance off. She had a frantic hope that the soldiers would take them for farm girls and pass them by.

But to the terror of both girls, the soldiers stopped in the middle of the road, then came to the fence and called out, "Seen any fellows lurking around here—or going toward the border?"

Teresa shook her head slowly, and her mouth dropped open a little as if she didn't understand very well. She looked around at Zita questioningly and saw that she too had a very clueless expression. "We saw a couple of fellows going up that way a while ago," Teresa heard her say in a dull, whining voice, pointing in the wrong direction.

Teresa quickly took up this cue. "It was more than a couple. You'd call it a bunch. They had big bundles, and we wondered where they were going so fast."

"Did you notice what they looked like at all?" asked the first of the soldiers.

"No, it wasn't very light. One was tall and one was—" she motioned to indicate broad shoulders. "I didn't notice much."

"Sounds as if it could be that Janos Nagy and the fellow that was with him," said one of the soldiers, looking much pleased. "Hadn't expected to get that much information. They look clueless enough, those two."

"Kind of pretty, though," said another. He gave the girls a laughing glance. "That's right, girls. Always keep your eye out for a good-looking fellow. Sorry we can't stay. Might come back later." And with farewell waves, the soldiers went quickly off in the direction the girls had indicated.

Though Teresa was trembling so she could hardly move, she shouted a command to the cows. They were willing enough to go to the barnyard, but it was evident their accustomed way led them by the strawstack, and they refused to be turned away from it today.

Teresa gave Zita an almost despairing glance, but Zita said, "It's a good thing, Teresa. Give us a chance to say a word or two to the boys."

Janos seemed to think so too, for as the girls drew near, he brushed some straw aside and put his face out of the little burrow he had carved near the ground.

The girls had plenty of eager questions, and he answered them rapidly. "Artur's here too," he said. "Sleeping now. We took turns."

"How did you get here so fast—ahead of us?" asked Zita.

"Got a lift part way by truck. Left our bicycles. We may have to stay here for the day, from the looks of things. Maybe you girls can get some food up at the farmhouse. That way you can find out whether they're friendly to us or not and maybe get some information about how things are around here. You did a good piece of work when you got those soldiers out of the way, for the time being at least."

Teresa would have liked to burrow into the strawstack and stay there until dark, her brother close at hand. But the boys needed food if they were to travel, and she and Zita had only a little left, sparing though they had been with it. And there was no assurance that even the strawstack would afford them safety now. Someone on the farm might well have caught sight of them, and the sooner they found out if the farmer was a friend or an enemy, the better.

The cows were making their own way to the barnyard, and the girls followed them. Teresa, her stick still in her hand, was trying to plan the best possible way to approach the farmer and talk to him when he suddenly appeared around the corner of the barn. He was a younger man than they had expected to see. He seemed greatly agitated and was scowling at them.

"And what do you think you're doing here?" he asked brusquely.

"Well—we're—we're driving the cows just now," faltered Teresa.

"You want a job milking?" demanded the man. "I don't know where you came from, but if you can milk, you've got a job. My wife's sick. I have to get back to her."

"I can milk," Teresa said eagerly.

"And I'm a nurse." Zita spoke in her old competent voice now that there was something she knew she could do. "Let me see if I can help your wife."

The relief in the man's face was swift and evident. "Come on then," he ordered, leading the way. "You can both get right to work. Those soldiers have kept on prowling around—" he almost spat out the words. "They scared her almost to death, or she would have gotten along all right. Couldn't get rid of them, even when I told them there was no one here—kept hunting around—"

The girls exchanged glances. This farmer certainly had no use of the soldiers. But there was no time to talk now. Zita was quickly shown into the house, and the man, returning a few minutes later, set Teresa to work milking.

She was thankful she knew how, even though the man plainly did not consider her very expert. "I'll have to help," he said in some disgust. Teresa's face fell, and he added more kindly, "You're not very big, but at least you're willing."

Zita was nowhere in sight when they carried the milk into the kitchen, and Teresa could see that the young farmer looked drawn and anxious. But then came a sudden wail, and a light broke over his face. "The baby! It's here! It's here! Thank the Lord!" he exclaimed and fairly ran into the next room.

The last two words reassured Teresa that this farmer was no Communist. Maybe he would help them. She looked around the kitchen, found bread and cheese and set it on the table, and soon Zita came out, pleased and excited, a baby in her arms.

"A fine little boy!" she said. "Is there warm water in that kettle, Teresa? And get me a basin, please. I'm going to wash him."

Teresa flew about, assembling the necessary articles, and watched with interest as Zita began her pleasant job. "Oh, isn't it a good thing we came here, Zita?" she exclaimed.

"I should say so!" agreed Zita. "She really needed us. Her

mother's coming, but with all the disturbance, the soldiers around and all that, she couldn't get here in time."

After that, there was nothing the young farmer wouldn't have done for them. The baby bathed, the mother made comfortable, the three sat around the table together, and the girls told something of their predicament.

The farmer's face darkened as they talked. "We'll help you outwit those—" He broke off and sat thinking for a few moments. Then a sudden, almost boyish grin broke out, and he hit the table with his fist. "I have an oxcart—I have a load of hay that should be sold—I think Ladovar would be a good place. You drive it there for me, and leave it at the marketplace with Gyula Renner. He knows me. Can you drive oxen?" he asked, looking suddenly at Teresa.

"Oh, yes. I've driven Grandfather's," she answered eagerly.

He nodded. "Good. You can pass as a country girl. Now here is what we will do—feed the boys out there in the strawstack, load them and the hay on the cart, and also this young lady." He smiled at Zita. "Some things you can do well," he said to her, "but you can't very easily pass as a country girl. This child here can. And it is better the two of you are not seen together."

"We have been seen together and would certainly be more easily identified as a pair," Zita said. "But I don't like to have Teresa sit there alone all day driving, while the rest of us are hidden in the hay."

"I don't mind. I don't mind at all," said Teresa eagerly. "It's a wonderful idea. And when we take food to the boys, we'll pick up the bundles and coats we hid under the bushes out there."

"Yes. And I can send you along on your journey with some food. If soldiers come here, I'll give them the wrong directions. My mother-in-law will soon be here. She will help."

This plan was promptly yet cautiously put into action, and soon an innocent-looking oxcart loaded with hay was ready to set out, a young but very alert driver holding the reins.

"This gives us good hope of reaching Ladovar today," Janos said.

"A pleasant and uneventful journey to you," said their host, and for his good wishes and his help, they thanked him heartily as they started off.

"Keep a sharp eye out," Janos said to his sister, "and give a good loud 'Haw' to the oxen if you see anything suspicious. Those soldiers have an unpleasant way, I've heard, of digging into hay carts with their bayonets to see if anyone's there." At Teresa's anxious look he added with a droll grimace, "For some reason they seem to want my company a lot more than I want theirs." And he gave her a jaunty wave before burrowing well out of sight.

It was like Janos to make light of it, but Teresa's hands were tense on the reins. About eight miles to Ladovar, the farmer had said. That was a long way by oxcart, over roads muddy with fall rains, and soldiers might at any moment appear and challenge her. Sitting there alone on the driver's seat, Teresa felt a great weight of responsibility.

As the oxen plodded along, Teresa's anxious thoughts flew ahead to the desired goal. After they reached Ladovar, they must somehow find their way to Szalay's farm. Even then, they would still be a good distance from the border, and Szalay's farm would be no more than a stopping place, she realized. But if they could reach it, she felt they would be well on their way to safety. And after that, all of them would be working together.

There would be Anyuka and wise old Bacsi and Ferenc, alert and daring, and Belo, the little brother who had shown himself so courageous these last days. But Teresa had to remind herself that there was no assurance they would be waiting at Szalay's. How she longed to know where they were and how things were going with them.

Chapter Eight

IF TERESA'S TROUBLED thoughts had flown many times to the other members of the little party that had set out together, Anyuka was even more anxious.

Indeed, she had scarcely been able to think of anything else from the moment she realized the two girls had been left behind. "Teresa and Zita," she said over and over that night on the train. "What will they do, Bacsi? Just two girls alone. What will they do? Teresa so young—so inexperienced—"

Belo reassured her. "Teresa isn't very young, Anyuka. She's fourteen, and in these last few days, she's shown a lot of sense. And Zita's grown up. I think they'll get through all right."

"There speaks youth," nodded Bacsi. "Perhaps the wisdom of a twelve-year-old is better right now than ours. It is at any rate confident." And in spite of her fears, Anyuka felt at least a little encouraged.

On reaching the end of the ride, she wanted to wait and see if the girls would not arrive soon. But when it was discovered that there was no schedule, no assurance whatever that Teresa and Zita would reach this place at all, Anyuka had to agree with Bacsi that it would be best to set off at once for Szalay's, hoping to find the girls there. But her heart was heavy.

Ferenc was blaming himself for leaving the girls on the platform in Budapest. "If I'd seen that they were left behind, I'd have jumped off," he said. "But I had all I could do to hang on without looking around."

Bacsi and Belo, though concerned about the girls, didn't waste time with regrets and worries. Belo was confident they would win through. And Bacsi had his hands full charting the best course to Ladovar and leading his little party, which had now been augmented by several other anxious wayfarers.

They must take advantage of the darkness to get as far as they could, Bacsi said, and try to find some sort of hiding place to rest toward morning. They set off, walking silently but rapidly along the road.

There was no one here to warn them of danger, but Bacsi realized from his previous experience that soldiers were likely to be lurking nearby. When shots rang out not far off, he said in a low voice, "We must leave the roads. We should strike a wood farther on. In the meantime, there may be swampy ground; so keep close together, and go very carefully."

Though they carried flashlights, they dared use them only sparingly, and the drizzling rain which began to fall added to the difficulty and discomfort of their progress. But through the drizzle and darkness, they plodded on, trying to keep together until at last Bacsi, who was slightly ahead, stopped with a low warning.

"Here's the swamp. We have to go through it. We can't go by the open road. Ferenc and I will feel our way as well as we can. You follow us."

"I'll take care of Anyuka," said Belo stoutly, and he grasped his mother firmly by the hand, while others who had joined the party clung together and pushed on, now and then finding a firm bit of footing, oftener sinking above their ankles in mud and water.

It was like a dreadful nightmare, Anyuka thought, as she tried to pull herself forward, mud sucking at her feet and holding her back at every step.

Some of the party gave it up, feeling that the risks of the open road would be preferable; others fell behind or decided to try to get to solid ground and wait until morning to go on. But Bacsi and Anyuka, Belo and Ferenc, anxious, if possible, to reach the rest of their party, went doggedly on, two or three young boys with them, until Anyuka slipped on a small hummock and gave a sharp involuntary cry of pain.

Ferenc was at her side in a moment, and he and Belo between them managed to get her to her feet. In the darkness they couldn't see that her lips were set in a thin, white line. Nor could they know how determined she was that no other cry should escape her to distress them and perhaps give away their whereabouts.

But Belo could feel her fist clenched, her arm taut. "What is it, Anyuka?" he asked anxiously, more frightened by the sudden cry which was so unlike his mother than by anything else that had so far happened.

"I think it is only that I have wrenched my ankle," she managed to gasp. "It may be you must go on without me."

"Fine chance!" said Ferenc, scorning any such idea. "Do you think we'd do that?"

"I'll follow later," she said. "A little rest, and I'll be all right."

"There's no place to rest here," said Bacsi, knowing as they all did that if they left Anyuka behind now, she would never reach the border. "We'll all help you."

"Yes, we'll take turns," said Ferenc.

"But I'll slow you up so," she objected. "You might never get there."

Once again it was Belo who hit on the best thing to say. "Anyuka, what would Janos do if we showed up without you? He wouldn't go on. He'd want to come back and find you. Teresa, too. And it's hard to tell what would happen then."

"Yes, yes," Anyuka had to agree. "But," she added despairingly, "I'm afraid I can't walk."

"Look here," said Ferenc. "We'll do the way we've done in games when someone was hurt. You've got one good foot. You put your weight on that, and I'll get on the side where the bad foot is. Then you hook your arm around my neck, and I'll hold you up and we'll go on."

"I'll take my turn too," said Belo eagerly. And the other boys quickly offered to do the same.

None of them knew what the struggle through the swamp cost Anyuka. But she realized that they would not go on, leaving her alone, and that Belo was right in saying Janos would not cross the border without her. That knowledge warmed her heart and gave her the strength and determination to fight her way through.

One boy after another came to her aid, and at last Bacsi, plodding ahead, paused to give the glad word, "Solid ground! We're through the swamp at last. Woods would be just a little way ahead now, and we can rest there and eat a little something. It's almost morning."

These words gave fresh energy to the weary travelers. The mention of food especially spurred the boys on.

Once far enough into the woods to feel some degree of safety, Bacsi stopped and the muddy and tired little company dropped thankfully down on the damp but solid ground. Anyuka bound up her ankle as well as she could with a strip torn from the cloth in which her bundle was wrapped while Bacsi handed out food.

Their meager breakfast over, they cleaned some of the thick layers of mud off their shoes and other clothing and then stretched out on the damp ground as close together as possible for warmth. The boys and Bacsi were asleep in a moment. Anyuka feared that her throbbing ankle and her anxiety for the missing members of the group would keep her awake; but exhausted as she was from the exertion of her journey through the swamp, soon she too fell asleep.

Through most of the day they slept. Ferenc, waking in midafternoon, saw Bacsi a little distance off among the trees, walking back toward the sleepers, and went quickly to meet him.

"I've been exploring," Bacsi said. "We're just about where I thought. We'll wake the others now and eat what we have left. Then we can go ahead through the woods, and by that time it will be dark enough to take to the open fields if not to the roads. I hope the rest has helped Anyuka. I wonder how she'll make it." He sounded somewhat anxious but added, "This, of course, should be much easier going."

"She'll make it," answered Ferenc confidently. "Even last night in the swamp she tried her best not to slow anyone up."

Ferenc was quite right. Anyuka asked the boys to find her a stout stick. Aided by this and by the boys, she got along at a better rate than any of them had thought possible, insisting that the ankle was much better today and only rarely agreeing to the frequent suggestions that they stop for her to rest.

"I want to get there! I want to make sure Janos and Teresa and the others are safe," she said so earnestly that Bacsi nodded, understanding how she felt, though he did try to suit the speed to her powers.

The way led through open country and though footing was more secure than on the previous night, there was now almost no protection from trees or bushes.

"I don't suppose we're likely to run into soldiers out here," Belo said.

"We can't be sure," answered Bacsi cautiously. "They could be traveling these roads to or from the border, where they're sure to be thick. For that reason we'd better keep to the fields."

"And not go too close to the farmhouses," added Ferenc. "Soldiers could be quartered there. How far do you suppose we have to go?"

"Around ten miles, if I have my bearings right. Even at our rate of speed," and he glanced at Anyuka, "we should make it before dawn, I would hope."

"And what if soldiers are quartered at Szalay's, what then?" asked Ferenc.

"We'll reconnoiter when we get there; that's all we can do."

On through the night they plodded, no one saying much, their thoughts often with the missing members of their families. Ferenc was anxious about his sister Piroska. Where was she, and who was helping her? And his father and mother—would he ever find them again? For his brother Artur, he had more hope. Artur and Janos were a resourceful pair. Anyuka was worried about Janos and Artur, and her concern for Teresa and Zita was even greater.

Now and then the group took the road for a little way to speed their progress, everyone straining to listen for sounds that might threaten danger, but mostly they went by fields, skirting the farmyards and buildings. Only occasionally did they venture to use a flashlight, but their eyes grew accustomed to the darkness, and the starlight aided them.

More than once, Anyuka felt she couldn't possibly go on, but the hope of finding Janos and Teresa and the others was a powerful pull onward. Yet in spite of all her efforts, she had to stop more often toward the end of the journey.

At last, far off, they heard the sound of chimes. "That must be Ladovar," said Bacsi softly, and their hearts lifted. "Now we must go very, very carefully," he warned. "It can't be far from here—half a mile perhaps. It may be that Szalay is known to be a sympathizer. It may be that they are keeping careful watch of his place."

"Let me reconnoiter," Ferenc said eagerly. "You tell me just how to get there."

"No, I had better go. I know the way and could maybe pass as just an old friend," Bacsi said. "You wait here. It's better for me to go alone." In another moment he disappeared into the darkness while the others anxiously waited.

Ferenc, as usual, found the inactivity hard to bear and longed to rush off into the night after his uncle. What if Bacsi ran into soldiers? What if he needed help? Ferenc touched his pistol, resolved that at the slightest sound he would go to the rescue.

But no sound came, and before the chimes had struck the next hour, Bacsi was back. "Coast seems to be clear," he said. His voice was low and guarded as he gave explicit directions. "Now follow me. We go first to the barn. There we find hay in which to hide if necessary."

"Are they there—the others?" Anyuka asked eagerly.

"I don't know yet. I didn't see Szalay. The house was dark. Time enough to rouse them when we get there. Come now."

Of all the way, it seemed to Anyuka that the last half mile was the hardest. Walking grew more and more difficult for her, but she was encouraged by Belo's eager whisper, "Anyuka, maybe they'll be there. And if they aren't, they'll come soon."

Bacsi and the boys longed to hurry. They were so near to at least comparative safety, yet they all knew soldiers might come out of the night at any moment and stop them. But they suited their pace to Anyuka's.

In the starlight they could at last make out the dim shape of a big combined house and barn, a great poplar tree out in front.

"It's all dark. How can we get in when we get there?" Ferenc whispered.

"Szalay promised to leave the side door of the barn unlocked," Bacsi answered.

Szalay had been true to his promise. The door yielded to Bacsi's touch, and in silent thankfulness the little company made their way into the shelter of the barn.

Once again the others waited while Bacsi slipped out and knocked very softly on the kitchen door with a prearranged signal. There was no response at first, and he had to knock more than once; but at last he heard a little sound in the kitchen.

"It's I, Bacsi," he said in a low voice.

The door opened cautiously, and a faint light showed a stocky man with a large nose and a jutting chin and a great shock of white hair.

"Come in," he invited.

"First, I get the others," said Bacsi, and with his heart fairly singing, hurried to bring the rest of the party.

"Come in," said Szalay once again. He stood aside while the little company filed into what seemed like heaven to them, though it was only a snug, warm kitchen with a good smell of cooking in the air.

"My wife—she knew if you got here, you'd be hungry. She's kept goulash ready," said the farmer, going toward the stove.

"The others—are they here?" was Anyuka's first anxious question.

Szalay paused in the act of ladling out the savory food. "The others?" he asked. "Are there others in your party? We haven't seen anyone else."

His wife came in now and was concerned to see that everyone was well fed and especially to make Anyuka comfortable.

Talk flew fast as the story of the flight so far was told. Then, with Szalay's help, they began to make plans for the final dash to the border. The last mile or two would be especially dangerous, he told them. Soldiers were thick there. Day travel would be impossible, and night travel was almost equally hazardous, for then flares were used.

"We mustn't stay here long," said Bacsi. "We don't want to bring suspicion and trouble on you."

"As to that—we'll stow you away in the haymow," said Szalay calmly.

"Anyuka we keep right here, in the best bed—rest her up and take care of that ankle," said Mrs. Szalay firmly.

Grateful as she was for the friendly help and much-needed care, anxious too about plans for the rest of the journey, Anyuka found it hard to keep her attention on the conversation. Her disappointment was great. She had been so sure that Janos and Teresa and the others would be waiting here.

Ferenc saw her concern and put his hand reassuringly on her arm. "Worried about the others, aren't you? They'll make it. You know Janos and Artur. Remember, they got a later start than we did."

"I know," said Anyuka and tried to smile at him. "But the girls! If only we knew they had someone to help them. And of course I slowed you all down with this ankle of mine. And you know, Ferenc, Janos always does things faster than anyone else. He and Artur should certainly have been here before now. Oh, Ferenc, I'm terribly afraid they've all run into trouble."

Chapter Nine

Teresa, driving her haycart along the country road, looked tranquil enough; but her heart was beating fast, and she was constantly on the lookout, ready at any moment to give the signal which would warn her passengers to stay very quiet and well hidden in the hay.

Eight miles to Ladovar, and never had miles seemed to stretch so long. She knew that soldiers might appear at any moment, and even if they did not, a new worry had begun to harass her. At the slow pace the oxen were plodding, could they possibly reach the village in time? The cart with its load of hay must be delivered into the hands of Gyula Renner himself. And if the marketplace had closed before they got there, how were they to get hold of Gyula Renner without wasting a great deal more time? Certainly they could not put the responsibility for returning the cart on Szalay, who would already be taking a risk in sheltering them.

Once or twice at the beginning of the journey, Janos had put his head out to give her an encouraging word or a bit of advice. Once he had said he was coming up to drive, but Teresa's voice was so sharp with fear as she refused the offer that he realized he was only adding to her worries by these efforts to help. So, like Artur and Zita, he settled down and was glad of the opportunity to get some rest and sleep before the final dash to the border.

A few foot travelers were encountered, two or three farm carts, and a food truck. Each time, Teresa watched them approach anxiously, resolved that if anyone stopped her, she would assume the clueless air that had served well before. But beyond a casual greeting given and returned, no words had passed; and in spite of the fact that they were drawing nearer the border, she began to feel a little safer.

Even though the sky was overcast, she could tell it was long past noon. It looked as if this part of the journey might be the uneventful one the young farmer had wished them. Thinking of their new friend reminded her of the food he had sent along, and she realized she was hungry and that the others no doubt were also.

They were going along between open fields now, and she felt there was small chance of anyone coming upon them suddenly. Glancing up and down the road to make sure it was empty, she delved into the basket of food, brought out bread and sausage, called softly to Janos, and handed him enough to share with the others. She finished her own lunch hastily, driving the steady old oxen easily enough with one hand. Though it seemed most unlikely that anyone would surprise them here, she kept a careful watch.

Then suddenly her heart was like lead, for from behind a strawstack came three soldiers, and they had their eyes on her cart. She had barely time to give the signal call before the soldiers stopped beside her with a sharp order to halt.

In spite of her fear, Teresa managed to assume an air of cluelessness, though her thoughts were racing. If only she had horses instead of oxen she might be able to make a dash for safety, but no use to try that. Just three soldiers—two of them quite young. Even if forced out of hiding, Janos and Artur would be a match for them if only they weren't shot before they could ready their weapons. But from the way the men glanced back at the place from which they had come, Teresa was sure that there were others there.

Harsh questions were hurled at her, but she only shook her head. Looking frightened took no effort; she managed also, with a partly open mouth and staring eyes, to look unknowledgeable, pretending not to understand. She had a fair knowledge of Russian and knew well enough that the soldiers wanted information about escapees. With the air of one who didn't quite know what they wanted but was willing to do her best to help, she pointed far back down the road with her thumb, hoping they would follow that lead.

"Janos Nagy?" one asked, and Teresa tried to suppress the sudden terror she felt. Somehow she managed to shake her head and give a careless shrug, muttering in Hungarian, "Two men," and pointing again in the direction from which she had come.

Two of the soldiers made as if to go, but the third—the older man—drew out his bayonet, and the glance he threw at Teresa told her plainly that he wasn't going to swallow any such story whole. Then, his jaw set hard, he jabbed his bayonet into the hay.

Teresa's agonized fear held her rigid and breathless for an instant. Then, in her desperate need, an inspiration came. She remembered that in Budapest the Russian soldiers seemed always hungry, and now she reached into her basket and brought out food.

With eager hands the two younger soldiers snatched at the bread and sausage she held out. To her intense relief, the other straightened up and grabbed for a share. But even as he ate greedily, he held his bayonet in one hand. Teresa sat there trying to keep from trembling, not daring to move without permission.

Another harsh question was barked out. Again she looked vague and, holding up the basket, handed them the last precious loaf. Whether this action mollified them or whether they thought it was useless to keep trying to find out anything from someone so obviously willing to help yet so clueless, Teresa never knew. She only knew that the older man said a disgusted word or two to the others that she understood to be, "Nothing there!" Then he waved her curtly on.

As Teresa drove on, she wondered anxiously whether that bayonet had done any harm. Then she realized that it couldn't have done more than give a scratch, for if it had really struck home, the soldier would have known someone was hidden there, however quiet that one managed to keep.

But she herself longed for some word that all was well. Some distance farther on, when Janos put out his head for an instant and said, "Whew! That was a narrow squeak!" she jumped and then almost laughed in her relief. "That bayonet came close enough to slit my sleeve. Another few pokes would have done the business. How'd you manage to get rid of them?"

"Gave them food and acted clueless," said Teresa. That problem was disposed of for now, but another was bothering her. Much as she wanted Janos to get back out of sight, she felt she had to get his advice first. "Janos, I know we'll be too late for the market and getting the cart to Gyula Renner there. What had we better do?"

"Go straight to Szalay's—that's all we can do. We'll manage to get the rig to Renner somehow. Do you know the way to Szalay's?"

"I've got Bacsi's directions. If we can just make it before dark, I'll be all right."

In spite of herself, her voice was anxious, and Janos said, "Want me to take over when we get a little closer?"

"No, I don't," said Teresa fiercely. "They're really looking for you, Janos. You get back in and stay there."

"You don't sound much like the clueless lump who fooled the soldiers," Janos said and withdrew his head. But as the afternoon wore on, he managed to keep a peephole open. In case his sister should need help, he wanted to be ready. To miss the turn that led to Szalay's might mean a serious delay.

The early twilight was drawing in, and rain began to fall. Janos was ashamed to be warm and dry in the hay. He wished he could leap out and take Teresa's place. But they were meeting more carts now, which told them that the farmers were coming home from market and Ladovar could not be far away.

"You're late for market," someone called out cheerfully. "We're all going home. Have trouble?"

Teresa nodded, and then, fearing the friendly farmer would come to investigate and offer help, she said, "Went out of my way. I'm taking it to a farmer tonight."

That was true enough, and the man called, "Success to you!" and went on his way. But the encounter diverted her attention from the road for an instant, and she would have missed her corner except for a warning sound from the hay behind her—Janos, giving the familiar call used to tell oxen to turn right. It was low and came just in time. Teresa turned into a little road that angled off to the right and gave a deep sigh of relief. How close she had come to missing the turn! But now she was sure she could find her way. She had memorized Bacsi's map and directions, and she knew Szalay's could not be far off. Another turn, and another. That must be it, just down the road—a comfortable farmhouse with barn attached, set on a hillside, a great tree out in front.

There had been some narrow escapes that day, but now they must surely be safe for the time at least. Then the disturbing thought that had occurred to Ferenc suddenly came to her. What if soldiers were quartered at Szalay's? It could easily be possible, so near the border.

"Brother!" she said softly, and Janos thrust his head out once more. "Soldiers may be there. You'd better stay hidden. When we get there, I'll get down and find out if I can. I could put on that clueless act again, if necessary."

"I was thinking of that," said Janos and added reluctantly, "all right, then. I guess it's about the only way. We don't want to get caught at this point after all we've weathered through so far."

Her heart beating fast, Teresa drove into the barnyard, jumped down, and ran through the rain and gathering darkness to knock at the kitchen door.

Mrs. Szalay answered, but Anyuka, who had been listening for that signal knock, came hobbling out of the next room, her face shining. The next moment, Teresa was clasped close in her mother's arms while both of them laughed and cried. "Thank the Lord! Thank the Lord!" Anyuka kept saying. "You've come! You're really here!"

"Janos and Artur and Zita are in the haycart," Teresa managed to say.

Ferenc rushed to tell the passengers in the hay that the coast was clear, to take care of the oxen, and get the hay under cover. Then they all gathered in the big kitchen while Mrs. Szalay put food on the table and everyone talked at once.

Wonderful as it was to have a warm, dry refuge, a rest, and a hot meal, all of them knew that they must get out of there as soon as possible.

"Tonight we must set out," said Bacsi. "We were waiting

and resting a little—Anyuka needed it especially. And we were hoping you'd get here."

"And now here we are," said Artur. "We can go on together."

Bacsi nodded. "We've been here since well before daylight. We mustn't endanger these good people any longer than absolutely necessary. They've already done enough for us—too much."

Szalay only shrugged. "So much any patriot would do," he said, and Mrs. Szalay nodded. "This is our part—we're glad to do it."

"Yes, and it's a big part," said Janos. "But we don't want to make trouble for you if we can help it. Your chance to help other people will be gone, too, if we bring suspicion on you. And of course soldiers might come almost any minute."

"What about the cart?" Teresa asked. She had driven the cart a good share of the day; it seemed somehow her responsibility, and she was anxious about it. "We must leave that with Gyula Renner."

"I'll drive it to his place if you'll tell me where he lives—and I'll do it right now," said Ferenc.

"Better let me see to it," offered Szalay, but the others would not hear of that.

"If you were seen driving strange oxen and a strange cart, neighbors or anyone on the road would wonder, and these days it is hard to tell who is on which side," said Janos.

"You don't know who may be watching, and you might risk your own safety and also your chance of usefulness in helping others," Bacsi put in. "If it is not too far, Ferenc could do it at once. He would likely be taken for a latecomer to market, the way Teresa was."

Belo begged to go with him, but everyone felt this would be an unnecessary risk; and Ferenc, with careful directions from the farmer, set off without delay.

"Now Teresa must get some rest," said Anyuka.

"Oh, I'm all right. I could start any time," Teresa protested; but she realized that Janos spoke good sense when he said she'd only make it harder for the others, and perhaps even add to the risks, if through sheer weariness she slowed them up.

"We've all had some rest today," Zita added her word. "Your turn now, Teresa."

"You folks shouldn't leave anyway till the rain is over, if possible," said Szalay.

Kind Mrs. Szalay took the girl in hand. Fairly stumbling with weariness, Teresa went into the next room and fell into a deep sleep almost before her hostess had drawn the covers over her.

She awoke to the sound of Ferenc's excited voice in the other room. "Soldiers all the way between here and the border," he was saying. "I was stopped all right, but my load of hay and an unknowledgeable look got me by. Gyula Renner is a good fellow, but he was uneasy about having me there, and I was anxious to get away. He told me soldiers were thick between here and the border, coming and going and watching the roads. I didn't see any on that little back road, the way he told me to get back here; but, believe me, I stuck to the ditches. That's what we'll have to do—that or take to the fields. Are there any woods at all?"

"Yes, some," said Szalay.

"We've gone over plans and ways pretty thoroughly," said Janos. "And now we'd better get out of here as fast as we can."

Teresa, coming quickly into the room, saw a cluster of tense faces, heard the farmer say, "Now have you all got it well in mind? About three miles and you're at the border. I've told you the safest ways and all the hiding places I could think of. Bacsi knows it from of old, but all of you should know."

"We *must* all know—every one of us," said Janos, and his solemn voice sent a shiver down Teresa's spine. "Let me repeat it for Teresa and all—I want to be sure I have it absolutely straight myself." As her brother slowly and clearly repeated the instructions, Teresa memorized every word.

"It is about three miles to the border," Bacsi said. "We must do our very best to keep together, but there is no telling. If we're separated, we must just try to keep going—do our best and get there somehow."

"We should have a signal," said Teresa. "It would be so easy to lose each other in the darkness. Our signals helped a lot today."

Janos nodded. "The hoot of an owl would be safe. Let's take that like this!" And he gave a low but good imitation, which each one echoed.

"Now, I think we've done everything we possibly can in preparation," said Bacsi. "We will start out in small groups for greater safety and wait for each other in the woods at the edge of the farm."

Only three miles! But as they said their thanks and good-byes and stole away from the sheltering farmhouse, all of them knew that the most dangerous part of the journey lay just ahead.

Chapter Ten

THE RAIN HAD stopped, but the wind was up, the scudding clouds still wild. There was only a little starlight to help the travelers, for they would not dare to use their flashlights in the open fields so near the house that had protected them.

Teresa and Ferenc and Bacsi, the first group to leave the farmhouse, crossed the field in safety and waited anxiously at the edge of the woods for the others.

It seemed a long time before the next group came silently up—Janos and Zita and Anyuka. There was another long wait, and at last they decided that the hoot-owl signal must be used. That guided Artur and Belo and the boys who had joined themselves to the party.

"Here we all are then," said Bacsi. "Now let us hope I can guide us to safety."

Half a mile through the wood—that was not too difficult, for here they dared to make at least sparing use of their flashlights.

But presently Bacsi gave the low-voiced warning, "Here we come to the open road."

"Wait a minute," whispered Ferenc. "They're using flares to light up the roads. You never know when they'll come."

"In case of flares," Janos said, "the only thing to do is to drop flat and stay there till the danger seems over."

"Might be best to keep to the ditches," suggested Artur.

"Safest anyway with soldiers on the road," said Bacsi.

But the ditches were so full of mud and water that progress there was all but impossible, and in desperation the little party took to the road—all except Teresa who had had one encounter with soldiers that day and couldn't quite bear the thought of another. Somehow she managed to stump along partway up the side of the ditch.

The roads themselves were muddy enough, the going heartbreakingly slow for the whole group, and the cold, gusty November wind they had to face increased their discomfort and added to their difficulties. But in their eagerness to get to the border and in their hope to reach it that night, they plodded doggedly on.

Zita voiced the hope of all of them when she said, "At least soldiers aren't likely to be out on a back road on a night like this."

The words were hardly out of her mouth when a sudden glare lit up the countryside. With the first flash, all of them dropped face down on the ground. Teresa, deep in the mud of the ditch, was sure her dark clothing and the mud would hide her even if soldiers came that way. But the mud was dragging at her, and she wondered how long she dared stay there. And what of the others? What of Anyuka with her injured ankle? Had she been able to drop down fast enough?

But now her concern for the others was forgotten, for she felt herself being sucked deeper into the mud. Her desperate effort to keep her face out so she could breathe took almost more energy than she could muster. She knew that soon she would have to call for help. Then, from far off, came the sound of shots. And after that she heard nothing more.

The others, edging toward the side of the road to keep out of the way of possible searching parties, knew nothing of her plight as they lay there waiting. But Szalay's directions had been good. No soldiers came down this small back road, and at last Bacsi gave the order to rise. "All here?" he asked softly, and one by one they checked in—all but Teresa.

"Tessa! Tessa!" Anyuka called in a low voice, using an old pet name for her, but there was no answer from Teresa.

A sudden fear swept over all of them. The mud there in the ditch was deep. What if Teresa had suffocated as she lay there?

"She's got to be there! We've got to find her!" said Janos.

To use a flashlight would be too dangerous, but he suddenly thought of how the soldiers had searched in the haycart earlier that day and, borrowing the stick his mother was using, he went down into the ditch and began carefully prodding.

He knew she must be there and didn't give up till his stick struck something solid. Then he reached quickly down and found his sister's coat sleeve. "She's here!" he exclaimed; but even as he spoke, his heart sank, for when he tried to pull her out, he received little help from her. "Boys! Come here!" he called softly.

Artur and Ferenc were there in an instant, and together they drew her out of the clinging mud that had covered her and carried her half-suffocated up to the road.

Zita and Anyuka knelt beside her, wiping her face free from mud and, with great thankfulness, heard her draw a deep, shuddering breath.

"I managed to keep my nose out," she whispered, "till the very last."

"Looks as if we got you out just in time," said Ferenc.

"Can you walk along all right if we scrape this thick mud off your clothes, Teresa?" asked Janos. "For that matter, we all have some mud to get rid of."

"Oh, yes, I can walk. I'm sure I can," said Teresa, managing to struggle to her feet with some help. "This time I'll stick to the road with the rest of you, soldiers or no soldiers."

But Bacsi said, "We don't dare go farther by road. This one soon turns into one that is more traveled. We must be pretty close to the border now. The flares show us that, and so do my calculations. Here we must take to the fields, and if you hear a hoot owl, that is a signal to stop this time."

Silently, they followed him. At first the going was harder than ever, for the fields were deep in mud and water and they had to pull their feet free with each step. But soon they were thankful that their wise leader had guided them into the fields. For searchlights began to sweep the road, and instinctively they crouched down and tried to go faster.

Teresa gritted her teeth and forced herself to keep up with the others, but she was grateful when Artur stopped to help her while Ferenc and Janos helped Anyuka.

With firmer ground under their feet at last, they began to run, and soon in the distance they could see the light of a campfire. Then came the soft hoot-owl signal, and they drew up short, waiting.

No one wanted to stop there. Danger was all around them, and the border very near. Ferenc wanted to make a dash for freedom, wild and desperate though the chance might be, and he knew the other boys felt the same way.

They stood in a huddled group, listening tensely, until Bacsi, who had been a little ahead, came back and said in hurried whispers, "I'm going on ahead to investigate. The campfire undoubtedly belongs to the soldiers. All the bridges are guarded, we know that. The soldiers, of course, are all Communists; but if they are Hungarian, I may be able to make some sort of a deal with them. They are not so keen to shoot their own countrymen or send them back home to be shot or sent away."

"Let me go," said Janos urgently.

"No," returned Bacsi firmly. "You are young, Janos. If we get through, you have many years ahead of you. I am old. And I have the far better chance. You they would almost have to shoot, and you might endanger all of us. To me they may listen."

Loath as he was to let Bacsi take the risk alone, Janos knew he was right, but he was thinking hard as Bacsi once more went silently away. No one wondered at it when he and Artur and Ferenc whispered together, for all of them had become used to conversing in this way, and their thoughts were on Bacsi and the final dash for safety.

Teresa's heart was pounding so she could scarcely breathe. After all the dangers they had struggled through, she couldn't bear the thought that they might be caught now.

Almost before they had dared hope, Bacsi was back. "Hungarian soldiers," he said briefly. "Just young fellows. They were willing enough to make a deal. They'll stroll upstream a little way, and we'll make a fast crossing. The only thing is, it's getting toward morning, and they expect to be relieved soon. If Russian soldiers take their place, that's a different matter."

With the light of the campfire to guide them, the party walked rapidly toward the bridge, Bacsi leading. Almost there he stopped, and for the first time, there was dismay in his voice. "The other soldiers are coming on duty," he said. "We must run for it."

"Artur and Ferenc and I are going to swim for it," Janos said swiftly. "We planned to do that, if necessary. The rest of you are a lot more likely to get over safely without us."

A sudden terror came over Teresa. In that icy water and the darkness, how could they make it to the other side? And what if the soldiers used flares to find and shoot them?

But Bacsi said, "You're right. Hurry!"

Zita could not keep back an anguished, "Oh, Janos!" Then she clapped her hand tightly over her mouth to keep from saying another word.

Anyuka said, "The Lord keep you." And the boys were running swiftly downstream, away from the bridge and the light.

Bacsi too broke into a run now, and even Anyuka managed to follow. Teresa forgot her weakness and fairly flew over the ground. So near to safety! They couldn't be turned back now!

Bacsi was on the bridge, crouching as he ran, and the others followed his example. Teresa's heart was in her mouth, for now there was a flare, shots rang out, and she heard a sharp cry of pain. But no one stopped running.

Then she heard Bacsi say, "Thank the Lord, we're safe!" Austrian ground was under their feet.

Teresa felt an almost overwhelming rush of relief and thankfulness. But then came the sound of shots again, and Zita exclaimed, "They spotted the boys with that flare. I know they did. They're shooting toward the river. I don't want to go on. I want to wait here for Janos."

"It would do no good," said Bacsi. "They went downstream. They won't come out here. We must make for the nearest shelter. Some of our party are badly in need of it. And the boys may be there before we are."

"Belo, does your leg hurt much? Can you walk all right?" Teresa heard her mother ask anxiously. It was her young brother who had given that cry on the bridge.

But his voice was steady now, though he spoke with an effort. "I'm all right. How far is it to that shelter? Zita can fix me up there and stop the bleeding, can't you, Zita?"

"I can do something right now," Zita said. And quickly tearing her scarf, she managed the most necessary first aid.

With Anyuka, Teresa, and now Belo finding walking difficult, it seemed a long way to the nearest town. But soon the gray light of early dawn helped them, and at last in the distance they could see lights and knew that if they could just keep going, they would find help.

"Looks like the town hall," said Bacsi. "I heard they were using all public buildings. We'll make for that."

With a final spurt of energy, they reached the building. Bacsi opened the door, and Teresa saw a woman coming to meet them.

"You have here some very dirty, weary guests," she heard Anyuka say in German.

"And hungry too, I have no doubt," the woman replied in the same language, which they all understood. "First, we will give you food—not much variety, but all you want. And later we'll find a place in another building where you can at least lie down on the floor and sleep. Then we will see if we can find clean clothing for you. But this boy needs help, I see, first of all."

In a dim corner by the stove, a very wet young man was kneeling, holding out a coat to dry. Anyuka and the two girls hurried toward him, their hopes high. But it was no familiar face that turned their way.

"I suppose you wonder about me," the man said half-defiantly, for now they could see that he was in uniform. "I'm a Hungarian soldier all right, but I can't fight against my own people anymore. I can't bear the way things are being done. So I jumped in and swam for it and just made it. Plenty of folks who've tried haven't been so blessed."

"But many have made it, haven't they?" asked Zita.

"Some of our party tried that tonight," Bacsi told him. "We hoped they might be here before us."

"Oh, yes, yes," the soldier said quickly, as if he regretted his words. "Many have, to be sure."

Zita's heart was heavy as she went to help care for Belo, but she was glad she could report to Anyuka that it was only a flesh wound and would soon heal. One son, at least, had crossed in safety.

By the time the boy was taken care of, hot tea was ready, and they all sat down to a meal of dark bread and cheese and oranges. In spite of her anxiety, Teresa thought she had never tasted anything so good. But her eyes kept moving about the room and toward the door, for little groups were arriving and others leaving, doubtless for the sleeping quarters the woman had mentioned.

"Maybe Janos and the others got here before we did," she said hopefully to Zita. "Maybe they've already gone to the sleeping place." But even as she spoke, she knew that wasn't likely.

Zita shook her head. "The boys wouldn't do that. They'd wait for us no matter how worn out they were," she said. "Anyway, I've described them and asked, just to make sure. They haven't been seen. But they told me there are friends on the lookout for anyone who has to swim the river."

"Maybe they've gone to another village," said Bacsi.

But now there was a commotion at the door, and someone burst in. "Come and help, some of you," he cried. "Someone called from down by the river. A fellow in there needs help—just about frozen. Maybe if we hurry, we can pull him out."

"Just one?" burst from Anyuka. "But there were three!"

There was no answer. The man and his helpers were running with all speed for the river.

Chapter Eleven

"I'M GOING TOO! I have to see!" Anyuka cried, but Bacsi laid a firm hand on her arm.

"Wait here," he said gently. "You would only need someone to help you along."

Zita and Teresa, completely forgetting their weariness, were speeding after the little rescue party. "Oh, it's got to be Janos! It's got to be Janos!" Zita was saying over and over.

"Yes and Ferenc too! Ferenc too!" said Teresa. "And Artur," she added.

It was plain that the men had had experience in this kind of rescue work, and the early morning light aided them. The girls saw them help someone from the river, set him on his feet, and with a man on each side, start him running toward the shelter house.

"They're making him run to get him warmed a little," said Zita. "I can't make out—"

"Zita, look! They're getting someone else out of the river!"

exclaimed Teresa. A second one was pulled out and started running toward safety; and the girls, hardly breathing in their tense eagerness, saw them draw yet a third from the river. This one was not able to walk, but someone had a board handy, and on this improvised litter, he was carried carefully toward the house.

"Oh, Teresa, the first is Janos!" said Zita joyfully. "I can tell for sure now," and she started back to the shelter to get things ready.

Teresa stopped only long enough to see that Ferenc and his helpers were the ones following, and then she raced to overtake Zita, eager to be the first to tell Anyuka the good news.

"Anyuka! Janos is coming—Ferenc too! And they're bringing Artur!" she cried out, bursting joyfully into the room.

Anyuka shut her eyes and drew a deep breath. "Thank the Lord!" she said. "Oh, Teresa, we've got so much to be thankful for!" She added firmly, "I'm going over there and help the boys." The boys needed help. Even Janos, who had fared the best of the three, was half frozen and scarcely able to speak. A hot drink, a quick rubdown, dry clothing, and food soon revived him.

Before long Ferenc, too, was able to talk. Artur would require more care; but he would recover, given a little time and nursing.

"If we could have swum right across, we'd have been all right," Janos said, "but they shot at us, and we had to go downstream to get out of their range. It was a long swim and ice cold, and Artur got a cramp."

"We're all lucky to be alive," Ferenc said.

"Now that we're here, what happens next?" Janos asked.

"First," said the woman in charge, "we send you across the street to sleep. You'll have a lot of bedfellows. We've put straw on the floor of the school gymnasium. Then, as soon as possible, we'll put you on the train or bus, probably for Traiskirchen near Vienna. There's a processing center there, and at some of the other camps too, with shipments of clothes and other things from America, and students and workers from all over. They'll help you on your way."

"Will we go to America?" asked Ferenc.

"That I can't say," answered the woman, shaking her head. "Many countries have opened their doors. Do you know that they call you the *Flüchtlinge*?"

"Fugitives," said Janos nodding, "and it's heartening to be so kindly received." But he didn't say anything about America; and Teresa, looking at him quickly, felt almost sure he had other plans.

"I hope we find our folks among the *Flüchtlinge* at Traiskirchen," said Ferenc. "Or maybe they're here," he added hopefully.

Bacsi shook his head. "I've looked—through all the rooms."

"No one is kept here long," said the woman. "You have a better chance of finding your people at the rest camps and processing centers farther on."

Artur had opened his eyes now, and though he must stay quiet where he was for some time, there was good hope he would soon be fit again. It was with thankful hearts that the little party, cleaned up a bit, warmed, and fed, crossed the street to the school gymnasium. They were far from the homes and familiar belongings they had had to leave so suddenly, their beds were just straw spread on the floor, but they lay down with a feeling of safety they had not had for many days. Though their future was still uncertain, their sleep was sound.

Teresa's last wish as she drifted off to sleep was that they could manage to get to America. Of course, everything there would be strange, and life wouldn't be easy, she realized that, but she felt there was a real hope of finding safety and happiness there. The Communist schools had tried to teach them otherwise; but she knew, from letters and reports friends had received, that life in America was good.

After the days and nights of danger, of straining toward freedom, it seemed wonderful just to feel safe and a little hopeful for the future; and she awoke after several hours of refreshing sleep with a feeling of anticipation.

Anyuka was already awake. Teresa, looking at her mother when she thought herself unobserved, was surprised to see that her face was both sad and anxious. "Anyuka," she said softly, "good morning."

"This is a strange time of day to say 'good morning,'" said Anyuka, trying to smile.

"We'll say it anyway," said Teresa. "So many good things on this journey happened toward morning. Now we're safe here, and no matter what the time of day is, it's really toward morning for us, isn't it?"

"I'm afraid my thoughts were turning backward, toward home and the old days when things were better," said Anyuka, "but bless you, child, you're right. We're facing a new day for all of us, I hope. Don't be disappointed if it all takes time. We have many, many adjustments to make."

"I know. But we're used to things not being very easy, Anyuka. Now we have at least hope of better things."

She was glad to see her mother give a real smile now, to hear her say, "Yes, yes. Hope—that is a great thing. And that we now have."

By this time Zita was awake. Across the room the boys still slept, but Bacsi had gone. They found him across the street a few moments later with Artur, who was almost himself again.

"I must wake the boys," Bacsi said. "I find that two buses will soon be leaving, and we must go on to make room for others who will be coming in here tonight."

"Here come the buses now," said one of the women in charge. "You had better hurry."

"Yes," urged Bacsi, shepherding them outside. "You folks get in. I'll rush and get the boys right over. They'll give you a hand, Artur."

"Let's wait!" said Zita. "I don't want to take a chance of being separated again."

But others were crowding eagerly forward; and in spite of themselves, Anyuka, Zita, and Teresa were swept aboard.

"Bacsi will see that they get the second bus," said Teresa. But the second bus too was quickly filled, and in a few moments, they were speeding way.

"Will there be another bus soon for Traiskirchen?" Zita called out to the driver.

"We are not going to Traiskirchen," the driver shouted back and mentioned a name that was not familiar to any of them. "Where the next will go, we can't tell. We just have to do the best we can."

There was a look of dismay on Zita's face, and she was very quiet. The others were quiet too, remembering that the woman who first welcomed them had said that the *Flüchtlinge* were being taken by bus or train to Traiskirchen or some other camp, wherever they could find room. How would they find each other again, among the thousands of refugees, if the boys were taken to some other camp?

At the new camp, they had another friendly welcome, and here they heard languages of all kinds. People had come from everywhere to help.

Once again they were served bread and cheese and hot tea, and this time they had something Teresa had never seen before, which the woman called "tangerines."

"We will have a hot meal for you before long," she said. "From America many supplies have reached us—clothing too.

And from other sources. We have zipper bags for you with soap and towels and toothbrushes and all such things from the United Nations. Many people are trying to help you."

"If they will just help us find our brothers and our friends," said Teresa anxiously; and Anyuka quickly told of how they had only today been separated again, after other separations and reunions.

"That we may be able to do too," said the woman. "Let us just wait a little. They may come here—many, many *Flüchtlinge* do."

But the day went by with no sign of the missing members of the party. Zita, restless and eager to be doing something, offered her services as a nurse and was quickly put to work. Anyuka, though eager to be of use, was persuaded to rest and take care of her ankle. All kept an eager eye on newcomers; and Teresa wandered about the camp, stopping here and there to talk, hoping for possible word.

It seemed to Teresa everyone was looking for someone. There were parties also who were being joyfully reunited, and from these she took heart.

Great activity went on in the camp, much coming and going. Some of the refugees were sent on to make arrangements for journeys to far destinations—Australia, Canada, the United States. Others would find homes in European countries. People, though sad at being uprooted from their homes and homeland, talked hopefully of a new life.

But in spite of themselves, Anyuka and the girls grew more and more anxious and despondent as days went by with no word from the missing ones. Red Cross workers, people in charge of the camp, now began to do their best with messages.

"Things are not very well organized as yet. It has all happened so fast, and people have come in such numbers. We have just had to do the best we can," one of the workers said to Anyuka.

"And a very good best it is," she answered. "What would we ever have done without this help? Believe me, we are thankful. But oh, we are so anxious to find our dear ones."

Then, one stormy evening, the door fairly blew open, and in came a group so covered with snow as to be almost unrecognizable. But Zita knew them. She flew toward them and a moment later was in the arms of the biggest snowman of all.

"We just got the message this afternoon," he was saying. "There was no transportation available this way today, so we walked. We think we have good news. We've found out more about going to America and believe the chances are good for those of us who want to go." Janos hesitated a moment, looking at Zita, and added, "We must wait a little and see. The important thing is that we are together again; isn't it, Zita?"

"Yes, oh yes," she said happily. "And no matter where we go or what we do, we're not going to let anyone separate us again."

"Right," Janos said firmly. "Let's get married right away, Zita, just as soon as we can."

"I've been thinking and planning the same thing, Janos—and some other things too," Zita answered. And Janos nodded as if he too had been thinking hard and making plans.

There was a joyful reunion that night, and tongues flew fast. The boys who had been companions on the journey were happy to rejoin their own group. Teresa, Zita, and Anyuka had made friends in the camp, and everyone was glad of their good fortune.

Zita and Janos were married in a quiet little ceremony two days later. The day after the wedding, Janos had some news for his family.

"Zita and I aren't going to America," he said. "We're going to stay and do what we can to help Hungary and our people. Thousands of them are trying to get across the border; maybe we can help them as we were helped."

Anyuka nodded. "You are right. I do not know how I can bear to leave you, but you are right. Here you can still help our people."

Teresa asked, "Won't you come to America at all?"

"I don't know. Maybe later, when there is nothing more we can do here. Then maybe we can do more in America—let the world know the truth about what happened in Hungary."

Anyuka took Janos' hand and looked up at him. Her face was sad, but proud too. "Do all you can, Janos," she said. "And in America we will be thinking of you and Zita and waiting for you."

Ferenc had news of his mother and father and Piroska. They were at another camp, and Ferenc was hopeful that they would all be together soon.

"Maybe we can go to America together," Teresa said, "your folks and us, Ferenc."

"As to going together, I can't say," said Ferenc. "But when we get there, we'll find each other, won't we?" His voice held a question and a promise that made Teresa feel a little shy, but very happy.

Parting was not easy, but they kept their spirits up by speaking hopefully of the time when they should meet again. Then Janos and Zita started to make their way back to the border, and the others went on to the next camp.

There were long days of waiting after that, and transfers from camp to camp; but one of the moves brought the travelers to the place where Ferenc's family waited.

Then at last one day came the long-awaited word; arrangements had been completed, and they were soon to fly to America. "And we're going on the same plane!" Ferenc told Teresa.

As the great ship rose and flew over the countryside, Belo, Ferenc, and the younger members of the party were filled with excitement. But Teresa saw Anyuka looking backward with a wistful glance at the land they were leaving.

"Maybe we can come back someday, Anyuka," Teresa said.

"Who knows? Things may change."

"Who knows, indeed," said Anyuka, and Teresa's spirits rose as she saw new hope and determination in her mother's face. "In the meantime, Tessa, we will have to work hard to build a new life. I am thankful I can sew. There must be work for a good Hungarian dressmaker."

"We'll have to learn English—an American girl at camp said they had special classes even for grownups. And she taught me a few words I can say right now, like 'Hi!' and 'How are you?'" Teresa hoped this would win a smile from her mother, and it did.

"How long will it be before we are there?" Anyuka asked.

"About fourteen hours, I think. Let's see—what time will that be—." Teresa counted the hours. Then her face lighted. "Anyuka, you remember what I said about good things happening to us in the morning? By the time we get to America, once again it will be toward morning."

More Books from The Good and the Beautiful Library

Trini, The Strawberry Girl
By Johanna Spyri

On the Edge of the Fjord
By Alta Halverson Seymour

Escape to Freedom
By Ruth Fosdick Jones

Steppin & Family
By Hope Newell

goodandbeautiful.com